MU00612529

The writer Samuel Johnson once wrote, "People need to be reminded more often than they need to be instructed." Randy Hain has provided a timely and precious reminder in *Upon Reflection*, a more valuable gift than anything new or novel could ever be.

—**Patrick Lencioni**, *New York Times* Bestselling
Author and President, The Table Group

In this wonderful book by my friend Randy Hain, you will learn the discipline of reflection. It is a powerful leadership habit that will not only improve your life at work, but have positive ripples through your personal life too! *Upon Reflection* gives you all the tools you need to lead better and be better. Read, study, and share this book with colleagues, friends, and family. We all need more reflection.

—**Chester Elton**, The Apostle of Appreciation
and *New York Times* Bestselling Author,
Leading with Gratitude and *The Carrot Principle*

Randy Hain's candor and transparency are desperately needed in the chaos of the modern world for busy professionals. *Upon Reflection* will inspire you to pause, reflect and think about practical choices that will change your behaviors for a more fulfilling and purpose-driven life.

—**Camye Mackey**, EVP and Chief People, Diversity, and
Inclusion Officer for the Atlanta Hawks and State Farm Arena

Randy Hain has delivered another must-read! I have seen Randy facilitate a strategic planning exercise with our Brock School of Business Dean's Advisory Board and can attest to his wisdom and keen insight on a firsthand basis. That wisdom permeates this book and is further evidence that Randy is a leading voice in helping organizational leaders understand the best and most effective ways to lead.

—**Charles (Chad) M. Carson, PhD**,
Dean and Professor of Management
Brock School of Business at Samford University

Randy Hain does it again! With his direct, compelling, and sincere writing style, Randy helps us understand the importance of balancing priorities in life to make the best of every experience, every interaction with others, and everything we do at home and at work. His many experiences as a business leader, professional, coach, husband, and father provide us with an effective guide on how we can be better professionals, engaged family members, better examples to our children, and, simply, better humans. Great work.

—**Juan Perez**, Chief Information Officer for Salesforce

What makes Randy Hain so extraordinary is his ability to focus on his topics with authenticity, intelligence, and wholeheartedness. Randy is a rare breed, and anyone who has the opportunity to meet him or read his book will be a better person for it. He is masterful in his writings and teaching.

—**Jo Ann Herold**, Author, former CMO at
The Honey Baked Ham Co., LLC and Interface

Upon Reflection perfectly captures the fine balance between theory and practice, between the ideal and the real. Randy Hain provides a genuine blueprint for creating harmony between the past, present, and future. Readers of all types will gain insights into the value of the examined life and ways to implement that collected wisdom.

—**Paul J. Voss, PhD**, President, Ethikos and
Associate Professor, Georgia State University

As a society, we have rightly begun to put greater emphasis on mental health over the last decade. *Upon Reflection* has much to offer toward this conversation as Randy explains in a compelling way how important it is for busy professionals to carve out time for reflection. It will leave you informed, pondering, and equipped for the mental rigors of our hectic world.

—**Darin W. White, PhD**, Margaret Gage Bush Distinguished
Professor, Chair, Entrepreneurship, Management, Marketing
Department, Brock School of Business at Samford University

Many people use vaults at the bank for keeping their precious treasures in safe-keeping. In this book, Randy Hain delivers to readers a vault full of priceless advice. Read it and cash in!

—**Virginia Means**, Chief People Officer,
United Distributors, Inc.

Randy Hain has done it again! *Upon Reflection* is a book for all of us—reminding seasoned veterans of what we believe but forget to practice and teaching younger professionals the timeless values and virtues that make for a healthy life and career. Randy serves as a sort of sage who equips us all to live our best life. I recommend this resource to anyone.

—**Dr. Tim Elmore**, Author, CEO, and
Founder, Growing Leaders.com

As a busy professional, reflecting on your experiences is so important. I appreciate how Randy shares his insights and personal experiences which you can apply to all aspects of your life. *Upon Reflection* offers clear insight on leveraging those experiences to growing as a leader. This is a book that I will reference every day.

—**Kyle Hamilton**, SVP of Field Operations for MetroNet

In a time when the world is looking for not only career advice but also advice to help guide your daily work, Randy Hain has delivered. *Upon Reflection* will ask you to slow down and go on a journey with Randy through his experiences, but it will also ask you to reflect on your past experiences and prepare you for the future. Randy has the gift of asking critical questions that you can use in your personal and professional life. I will give this to friends, family, and teammates.

—**Ben Milsom**, Chief Ticketing Officer,
Tampa Bay Buccaneers

Randy Hain has a "come alongside" writing style that naturally mirrors his mentoring and coaching. *Upon Reflection* addresses real life issues with a practical and relational approach. Randy's ability to extract meaning from everyday experiences brings an injection of wisdom to every chapter. Read this book and buy one for a friend.

—**Steve Moore**, Author, *Grow Toward Your Dreams*,
president of nexleader and Growing Leaders

If you ever need a reminder that there is still humanity in this world, then this is the book for you! *Upon Reflection* comes at just the right season for our entire society. In our current world of fast-paced living—filled with shallow relationships, hurried activities, and unfiltered conversations, Randy Hain presents fresh perspectives to help us live more meaningful lives of purpose, intentionality, civility, and kindness. He does a masterful job of explaining the discipline of personal reflection while offering practical tips on how to get better at this skill every day!

—**Ash Merchant**, President and CEO, Lionheart Partners

Generosity, gratitude, kindness, vulnerability, self-reflection, courage and appreciation. . . . If these words are meaningful to you, then this book is a must-read. *Upon Reflection* captures the true essence of what is vital to being an impactful human. Thank you, Randy Hain, for sharing your gifts with all of us to help us better ourselves and bring out the best in all of those we have the opportunity to influence in our personal and professional lives. This timeless book is a powerful resource.

—**Fran Mallace**, CEO of Make-A-Wish Arizona

In *Upon Reflection*, Randy Hain invites us to take a short break from our busyness and to pause, reflect, and think. If you accept the invitation, you will be rewarded for doing so. Randy combines his vast lived and shared experiences with his compelling storytelling to provide insights that transcend the distractions that are part of our day-to-day. As he does in his coaching and consulting, he then translates those insights into practical and actionable tools to guide the journey toward a more effective and rewarding approach to work and life.

—**Joseph Blanco**, President, Crawford and Company

Once again, Randy brings timeless wisdom to both our personal and professional lives. Especially in today's day and age, we need to remind ourselves of these lessons that provide the framework for a thriving life. This is a shareable resource for co-workers, our children, and our children's children.

—**Ray V. Padron**, CEO, CI-Brightworth

I really love how in this, Randy's ninth book, he challenges the reader to not only reflect on the insights he shares but also provides practical steps to put those reflections into action. The one that struck a particular chord with me was how to foster civility through mutual respect and open dialogue on topics that are so divisive in our society. Doing so takes courage and being willing to accept that the conversation will not change another's point of view, BUT you have the conversation anyway. Thank you, Randy, for these lessons.

—**Pat Falotico**, VP, Client Development for Pathbuilders

I've partnered with Randy in one way or another for many, many years, and when I read this book, it brought together the themes we have discussed often and at length. I was particularly drawn to the third section, "Being Good Humans." As someone who built a career around strategic communications, I feel this gets to the literal heart of the matter. Business is human because business is people, and when we respect one another at that basic level, things become easier and more fun. We live one life, after all.

I love this line: "We have a clear choice to make about how we engage with one another, and there is no reason why we can't choose civility, kindness, respect, and even love in our daily encounters." Any one of us can be a voice of calm and reason in our divided society, to lead with respectful dialogue and an aim to understand even if we don't agree. We can "be like Dave"—what a great story in this book. Thank you, Randy, for always bringing the point home so poignantly.

—**Lisa Bigazzi Tilt**, CEO, Full Tilt Consulting

Randy Hain has done it again! His penchant for being able to relate experiences, provoke thought, and guide us toward intentional implementation of action in a practical and meaningful manner is second to none. Randy shares this uncanny gift with all of us in his latest book, which spotlights the incredibly important and necessary act of reflection.

Randy is one of the most authentic people I have been lucky enough to know. He has integrated these practices into his own family, work, and spiritual lives, which makes his teachings so genuine. What makes the book so appealing is that it is applicable to all of us: old, young, fathers, mothers, brothers, sisters, etc. He writes with such an easy, flowing, and understandable flair that you will have trouble putting it down. Such great life lessons!

—**Patrick O. McNulty**, CEO, St. Vincent
de Paul Society of Georgia

Upon Reflection is a must-have resource. Randy's authentic and simple storytelling style hits home at a deep level. Not only are the lessons in the book timeless, but they are also timely. Everyone in every season of life can apply the wisdom shared in the pages of this book. *Upon Reflection* provides an accurate and much-needed compass for helping busy professionals navigate the craziness of life.

—**J.T. Thoms**, Speaker and National Account
Executive for Jackson and Coker

Randy Hain excels in weaving stories to share relevant, practical insights and the wisdom he has gained as a husband, father, and executive leadership consultant. Early in my career, I was driven by ambition and a calendar that was too full and too unfocused. What I needed was time to reflect and become more self-aware. What I needed was Randy Hain's newest book, *Upon Reflection*. Through the stories Randy shares, you will learn how to slow down and reflect, learning from what you do, but more importantly, learning about who you are and the people whose lives you impact. Who we are is much more important than what we do. *Upon Reflection* will help you achieve success in all areas of your life.

—**Michael Bickerstaff**, President, Virtue@Work

UPON REFLECTION

Helpful Insights and Timeless Lessons for the Busy Professional

Randy Hain

Author of *Essential Wisdom for Leaders of Every Generation*

SERVIAM PRESS

Copyright © 2022 Randy Hain

All rights reserved. With the exception of short excerpts used in articles and critical review, no part of this work may be reproduced, transmitted or stored in any form whatsoever, printed or electronic, without the prior written permission of the publisher.

ISBN: 978-1-7377244-2-1 (softcover)
ISBN: 978-1-7377244-3-8 (e-book)

Published by Serviam Press, LLC
www.serviampress.com

This book is dedicated with love and gratitude to:

Stella Maris

*Thank you for being my North Star and guide
on the journey to write this book.*

CONTENTS

Introduction

People often ask me how I am able to write on such a wide variety of topics in my blog posts and books. I think it's because I have a lot of interests and never really set out to write anything brand-new, but instead try to pause and reflect on my life and work experiences as often as I can. Life is plenty interesting with lots of variety if we slow down and thoughtfully ponder successes and failures, lessons learned, and the meaningful encounters we have with the people who cross our path each day. In my experience, the greatest contributor to my personal growth has typically been derived from gazing into the past with a desire to learn and apply the lessons I glean versus peering into the future and seeking what's next.

The busy professionals I know, spanning all generations in the workforce, tend to focus the vast majority of their attention and time during the workday on racing from task to task and meeting to meeting in a frantic rush to complete ever-growing to-do lists and simply getting their jobs done. The typical workday is often about coping and surviving instead of growing and thriving. This is largely understandable and part of modern business, although I think many of us would change our approach to work and our careers if we knew how.

My previous book, *Essential Wisdom for Leaders of Every Generation*, was a practical collection of actionable ideas and best practices to equip leaders and aspiring leaders to thrive in work and life. My ninth and newest book, *Upon Reflection: Helpful Insights and Timeless Lessons for the Busy Professional*, also offers an eclectic mix of actionable and practical ideas on a number of relevant business topics . . . and something very different. In this work, you will observe that each chapter is written through the lens of reflection. I share authentic experiences, lessons, triumphs, and failures on various business and life topics to provide useful and practical tips you can use, but also to demonstrate the power of thoughtful consideration and contemplation in a way that I hope will help you model this helpful practice in your own life.

The book is divided into three parts and covers a wide range of topics, as you will observe in the Table of Contents. In Part One: Learning from the Past, we undertake a journey together to examine pivotal moments and profound lessons from my life and the lives of others to share valuable insights that will benefit professionals at any stage of their career. In Part Two: Practical Lessons for the Busy Leader, we tackle several thought-provoking topics relevant for today's busy professionals and offer actionable best practices on these topics you can immediately put to good use. In Part Three: Being Good Humans, we explore true stories, powerful lessons, and practical concepts to help us show up as better humans in today's world and counter the negativity, anger, and divisiveness that has become so prevalent. This section has clear relevancy for businesspeople, but it is also 100 percent relevant for all of us who journey together as fellow travelers in this world, regardless of our occupation or stage of life. As is my typical writing style, all of the chapters in *Upon Reflection* are relatively short, practical, actionable, and designed to open wider the aperture of your thinking.

I wrote *Upon Reflection* through my lens as an executive coach, leadership consultant, husband, father, and community servant. Before I became an executive coach and consultant, I spent more than twenty-five years in executive roles, including senior operations leadership for a national retailer, vice president of people for a $2 billion national restaurant company, and later as the managing partner of a well-respected executive search firm. I have also been fortunate to serve on a number of nonprofit boards and give my time to a variety of wonderful causes. The rich experiences I am grateful to have had during my life as well as my daily engagement with professionals from around the world often informs my writing, and that is certainly the case with this new book.

My hope for the readers of this book is that you will more frequently pause, reflect, and think. I encourage you to block distractions that make you lose focus and improve at both living in the moment as well as reflecting more on the past. Practically speaking, try to pause between meetings and reflect on what has happened since your day began.

- Who have you met?
- How can you help others around you?
- Where can you make a positive difference at home, work, or in the community?
- Are you on track with your work goals or do you need to course-correct?

- As you reflect on yesterday, last week, and even ten years ago, how does the past inform and influence your present?
- What are the valuable lessons you have learned and how do you apply them to your daily life?

Of course, almost everything you will glean from *Upon Reflection* applies to helping you in your personal life as well as your business life.

How do you become more reflective? It takes patience, practice, intentionally, self-discipline, and possibly years to perfect. Stay with it and don't give up. Get started now and know that reflection is for everyone, regardless of age or occupation.

What are some tools and ideas to help you become more reflective? Here are **four suggestions**:

1. **Develop the habit of journaling.** I have used a journal for over two decades to capture my random thoughts, observations, and reflections and always have one with me. I have filled up twenty-three journals since I began the practice.
2. **Schedule a window of quiet time on your calendar every day when you are sharpest and will have the fewest distractions.** My preferred window is 6:00 a.m. to 7:00 a.m. over a cup of coffee.
3. **Integrate reflection with exercise.** I find my daily work-out and two-mile walks at the end of the day are ideal times to practice reflection.
4. **Practice being more present.** Proper reflection is stimulated by memories created from time when you are truly present with friends, family, colleagues at work, alone

with nature, or doing anything healthy, productive, and meaningful.

This book is the useful fruit of my own ongoing commitment to reflection. As I grow older, I can share without a doubt that my life is richer and fuller because I make time for this. I truly hope you find *Upon Reflection* helpful and the catalyst for a newfound focus on reflection in your own life.

PART ONE

Learning from the Past

CHAPTER 1

Savoring the Moments

You must live in the present, launch yourself on every wave, find your eternity in each moment. Fools stand on their island of opportunities and look toward another land. There is no other land; there is no other life but this.

HENRY DAVID THOREAU

As I was pulling together the chapters for *Upon Reflection*, I thought about a recent family vacation out West and our visits to the Grand Canyon and Sedona, Arizona. This part of our great country is breathtaking, and everywhere we looked around us on that trip, we were usually gazing at something so beautiful that it looked like a painted canvas from a master artist. We had a wonderful time filled with great memories, and it was one of my favorite experiences with my wife and sons. None of us wanted it to end. I also thought, with considerable regret, about all the missed opportunities in my life to savor moments like this when I was younger.

In my early twenties, I was living the impoverished life of a new college graduate trying to get established in my career. I was lucky to experience the occasional three-day weekend, much less a relaxing vacation. In my late twenties I got married and was enjoying more career success, but I struggled to truly enjoy and be present for the trips, vacations, and quiet moments with my wife as I had difficulty at times blocking out thoughts of work and all that awaited me when I returned to the office and my hectic job.

Our sons came along in my early thirties. I was becoming calmer, but I still struggled to relax and live in the moment with my young family. My saintly wife always made sure we had fun vacations, and we spent a lot of time together, with family dinners and weekend activities a priority. But I still found myself frequently checking email, thinking about that unresolved work issue, or how my team was going to make our revenue goals when I should have been focusing that time and attention on the people I loved most in the world.

In my late thirties and early forties, I began to realize something quite profound that I wish I had learned much earlier in my life: *My job exists to serve my family; my family doesn't exist to serve my job.* When that thought began to sink in and truly take hold of me, it became the catalyst for significant changes in my life that took years to fully settle in. I learned how to leave work at the office and not bring it home with me. I realized that worrying about business-related problems during nonwork hours was not helping to solve them any faster. Instead it only caused me unneeded stress and anxiety, which then negatively affected my family.

I often share with my clients that *time is a finite resource, and we have to manage it well.* That idea occurred to me many years ago as I was going through the evolution in my thinking about making sure my job existed to serve my family. I realized that every moment with my loved ones and friends was precious, and

I could no longer take this time with them for granted. I call this *living life in real time.*

I am now in my mid-fifties, my wife and I have been married for almost thirty years, and my sons are in their twenties. My oldest son has high-functioning autism and lives with us. Our youngest son is a senior in college. With intentional effort, determined focus, and many missteps along the way, I feel I have learned to properly savor the important moments in life. I still love the work I am privileged to do and give it my best effort, but I have learned to turn it off when I need to and make sure it doesn't have an adverse effect on the people I care about most.

I am sharing this insight into my personal journey because I frequently meet professionals of all ages who are experiencing the same challenges I have encountered. It's important for all of us to pause, reflect, and think about what matters most to us—and I sincerely hope work is not at the top of that list. We can excel in our careers *and* still excel in life. You don't have to choose one over the other, and don't let anyone convince you otherwise.

Practical Tips

Here are **five best practices** to consider if you feel your priorities are out of whack:

1. **Make a list.** What are your priorities? What matters most to you personally and professionally? Think about family, friends, faith, your health, serving great causes, experiencing beauty, and doing meaningful work. Create a blended list that covers everything in your life that matters to you.
2. **Audit and reflect.** Review your calendar for the last few

weeks. Work will likely take the majority of your time during the week, but where do the other nonwork priorities from the priority list you made in step one fit in? As you do this calendar audit, honestly reflect whether you were truly present in the nonwork moments or were distracted by work (or something else).

3. **Turn off your devices.** One of the biggest temptations is to let work and other distractions creep into your personal or family time by having your phone on and by checking emails, texts, or social media. Try going device-free from time to time, especially when you are with loved ones or friends. Be present and make them the priority.

4. **Be intentional and ask for accountability.** Schedule intentional time on your calendar to relax, exercise, read, listen to music, or recharge. Ask someone you trust to hold you accountable with how you are doing each week. Schedule intentional time with friends or loved ones. Give them your phone or turn it off and ask them to call you out if you seem distracted.

5. **Consider embracing a healthier version of FOMO.** Fear of Missing Out is a widely panned behavior that likely affects many of us to some degree. What if we look at FOMO differently? What if we "fear" missing memorable moments with our friends and families? What if we "worry" about not maximizing meaningful experiences in our lives? What if we become more concerned that work may be the most important thing in our lives?

I assure you I don't have all the answers about achieving the perfect balance of life and work, but I do have experiences and insights I hope will benefit those who read this book. I'll leave you with one particular memory of our vacation in Sedona. It was our last full day, and we were watching an incredibly beautiful sunset from a solitary vantage point in the hills around the city. I stood there and remembered vividly every moment of that special final day of our vacation capped off by one of the prettiest views I have ever seen. My family and I watched in silent awe as the sun went down behind the mountains, and I know we all felt an unspoken sense of gratitude to be together in that specific moment. Savoring that moment of beauty with people I love was all I thought about . . . and work never even crossed my mind.

Before going on to the next chapter, reflect on one of your favorite moments with your family or friends. Savor that memory for a few minutes and think about why it was so special. Why did you choose this memory? Most importantly, can you begin planning another opportunity to create a similarly powerful moment in the weeks and months ahead?

CHAPTER 2

Too Many Influencers in Your Life?

[Research] suggests that what we think of as free will is largely an illusion: much of the time, we are simply operating on automatic pilot, and the way we think and act—and how well we think and act on the spur of the moment—are a lot more susceptible to outside influences than we realize.

MALCOLM GLADWELL,
BLINK: THE POWER OF THINKING WITHOUT THINKING

During one of my recent afternoon walks at the beginning of the summer, I encountered several middle-school girl soccer games in progress on the local school playing fields. As I walked by one of the games, I observed several of the parents and the coach directing the players on the field. The coach, who seemed quite knowledgeable, was almost being drowned out by the well-meaning moms and dads encouraging their daughters to "get the ball," "score a goal," and "play defense." The confused look in some of the players' eyes because of so much conflicting direction was a bit comical . . . and oddly familiar.

I often encounter professionals at all stages of their careers who are overwhelmed with somewhat contradictory voices in their lives. In addition to mentors, coaches, family, and friends, the noise from social media, mainstream news, politicians, and influential celebrities can be confusing and toxic if not streamlined and harnessed in an effective way. To whose voices, if any, should you listen?

Through the introduction of a mutual friend, I met with a struggling senior leader a few years ago who proudly told me he had an executive coach, a life coach, a mentor, a therapist, and was considering finding a communications coach. My head was spinning at the thought of all these voices speaking into his life, and I asked him if this approach was effective. He looked at me strangely and then said he thought so but wasn't sure. He then proceeded to share a business problem he was dealing with and asked me for advice. I helped him as best I could, but also asked him for his permission to share an observation. I respectfully told him I thought he had too many influencers in his life. I encouraged him to think about what he really needed in this stage of his career and streamline the number of people whom he sought out for advice.

He seemed nervous and a bit frustrated, but after a few minutes, he acknowledged that he had likely gone overboard with what he described as an addiction to having "lots of pros" in his life. We talked about his self-confidence, and he admitted it was low. I agreed to have a monthly call with him at no charge for a few months, but only if he would begin trying to stand on his own and let go of some of the people giving him counsel. Our calls were mostly me encouraging him, asking him tough questions, and challenging him to make decisions, as I could quickly tell he knew the answers and was more skilled and talented than he allowed himself to believe.

This leader eventually got back on track, not because of my coaching, but because he began to have confidence in himself and remove most of the well-meaning but often enabling and contradictory voices in his life. He began trusting his gut and own instincts. We still touch base over coffee now and then, and he encouraged me to share his story as a cautionary tale to others who may have fallen into the influencer trap.

If you are trying to discern who can and should be the key influencers in your life, consider reflecting on these **nine key questions**:

1. Am I clear about what I really need?
2. What are my strengths?
3. Where do I want to improve?
4. Who will challenge me and be unafraid to tell me what I may not want to hear?
5. Who can teach me new skills I wish to learn?
6. Who has walked down a path that I also wish to follow?
7. Who can I trust to allow me to open up and share my authentic thoughts and feelings in confidence?
8. Who shares my values?
9. Who will ask me tough questions and force me to solve problems rather than give me the answers?

This is not the definitive list, but it is a good list to get you started with your discernment process.

The recent encounter with the girls' soccer game and the senior executive experience from years ago made me think back to the lessons I have learned in my own life and the process of discernment I went through to determine who would be the most helpful and positive sources of influence for me. My parents have always been a source of wisdom, for which I am grateful. My wife has also served as a wise and insightful voice throughout our long marriage. Early bosses and mentors who took me under their wing and helped shape me as a professional have a fond place in my memory. Since the beginning of my career, I have gravitated to friends and professionals who possessed and modeled the skills, values, and virtues I admire and wish to mirror in my own life. I find peace and direction in the practice of my faith, as I listen for the subtle voice of God in my daily prayers and those who He places in my path each day. Sometimes, simply taking the time to reflect on my past experiences can be a source of helpful wisdom as I ponder different ways to handle situations and get myself back on track when I struggle. There are days when a chapter in a helpful and timely book recommended by a friend is all I need to correct my course or experience needed growth in a certain area of my life.

This chapter may not seem relevant to where you are in your life right now, and that's OK. But, if you have a suspicion that you have too few or too many influencers or the wrong voices speaking into your life, Know that it is possible to make the necessary adjustments. Review the questions I shared and get clear about what you require in your life right now and then be intentional about finding the resources you need. Consider the experiences I've shared from my life and see if they resonate with you and spark useful ideas.

We all need help from time to time—just make sure it is the help you really need.

Reflect on this chapter for a few minutes. Make a list of all the influencers from whom you get help, direction, or counsel of any kind. Use this chapter to help you discern if you have the right list and make the necessary adjustments.

CHAPTER 3

When Leaders Embrace the Abundance Mindset

The more principle-centered we become, the more we develop an abundance mentality, the more we are genuinely happy for the successes, well-being, achievements, recognition, and good fortune of other people. We believe their success adds to . . . rather than detracts from . . . our lives.

STEPHEN R. COVEY, *PRINCIPLE-CENTERED LEADERSHIP*

I was thinking not long ago about my mother, Sandi, who passed away in 2009. One of the many things I loved and admired about my mother was her generous nature and desire to help everyone she met. What you may find interesting is that she worked very hard in her full-time job as well as in her more important roles as wife, mother, sister, daughter, and church volunteer while enduring numerous health-related issues in her later years. My mother dealt with all the stress, illness, and adversity in her life with joy and a smile . . . and never complained. In fact, she was always *grateful* and saw her challenges as blessings, not burdens. She always had a kind word for others or some sort of encouragement to offer in spite of what might be described as overwhelming burdens to carry. It was through the way she joyfully lived her life that my mother taught me what living with an *abundance mindset* means, and her example has helped shape me as a leader, husband, and father.

I encounter people every day in my professional and personal life who exhibit either an abundance mindset or a *scarcity mentality*, which is the opposite of abundance. Leadership guru Stephen R. Covey initially coined these terms in his bestselling book, *The 7 Habits of Highly Effective People*. Scarcity mentality is about seeing life as a pie, so that if one person takes a big piece of your pie, that leaves less for everyone else to enjoy.

It seems that in the business world, many of us who are fortunate to be leaders have been conditioned to have a scarcity mentality. When we feel overwhelmed by the demands of our calendar, the challenges of finding good talent, an unexpected pandemic, or the normal stress of life, we may find ourselves in self-protective mode, being stingy with our time and hoarding our resources. We may be reluctant or unable to see our opportunity and obligation as leaders to look beyond our own problems to show kindness and encouragement, to generously share of ourselves with others, to motivate or inspire. A scarcity mentality may be keeping many of us from achieving our goals and the success we may crave, but more importantly from experiencing the richer, fuller, and more noble life the abundance mindset can offer.

Two Examples

A few months before I finished writing this book, I had the

opportunity to experience clear examples of the abundance and scarcity approaches in the same day. My oldest son, Alex, has been employed as a part-time employee for over six years by a global retail company at one of their stores near our home. Alex came down with COVID-19 and had to miss work for the first time in six years. I called the store to let them know Alex would be out of work while he recovered. The assistant store manager was very kind during our brief call and conveyed his hope for a speedy recovery.

Within five minutes of that call, the store manager called, and my wife answered the phone. He spent twenty minutes with her, asking about Alex, informing her that Alex would be paid for the hours he missed, and sharing how much he and the entire team valued him. He also shared a few specific stories about Alex's hard work and how much respect he had for my son.

What makes this story remarkable, and a good illustration of abundance, is that this gentleman was under enormous stress. His store, one of the busiest in the company, was understaffed, impacted by supply chain issues, and a recent COVID outbreak had significantly impacted his remaining team. Despite all of this and the burdens this leader carried, his first thought was to call the family of a part-time employee and show kindness, encouragement, and gratitude. He operated from a place of abundance when he easily could have wallowed in his scarcity.

Later that same day, I had a call with a business leader who was interested in me working with her and her team. I learned on our call that the team had experienced high turnover and was dealing with a host of challenges that were exacerbated during the pandemic. I also heard from this leader how busy she was with seemingly no control over her calendar, the long hours she worked, stress she was feeling at home, and how much she disliked her boss. It was also her perception that the team complained a lot and wanted more time from her than she could afford to give. I took all this in and asked for her permission to share an observation.

I respectfully challenged her that she was operating out of a scarcity mindset that was negatively impacting her team and her personal performance. We walked through possible steps she could take to reclaim her calendar and build air into the schedule, which would help her to invest in the team and elevate her leadership to the abundance mindset.

To her credit, she realized during our conversation that she had become somewhat blinded by her own significant challenges and had lost sight of her obligations as a leader to invest in her team. I share this example with her permission, and we kicked off a coaching engagement a few weeks later.

Always Show Up with a Gift . . . and Other Helpful Ideas

As you think about your desire to lead with an abundance mindset more consistently, I would like to share **four helpful ideas** to reinforce "abundance thinking":

1. **Always show up with a gift.** From the time I was a little boy, I remember my mother's frequent advice to "always bring a gift and never show up empty-handed" when meeting with someone. I used to think she meant only tangible gifts like flowers, a book, or a plate of brownies. As I grew older and watched her in action, I began to

realize that her brilliant advice meant so much more and included sharing gifts of kindness, encouragement, candor, connections, mercy, forgiveness, gratitude, good counsel, and inspiration with everyone we meet in our business or personal lives. I learned to never show up empty-handed and always be willing to share my gifts.

2. **Be grateful.** Always live and lead with gratitude. When we operate with a grateful mindset, we better appreciate what we have and are more inclined to share with others. This attitude of gratitude should also extend to appreciating our burdens and challenges, not just our blessings and good fortune.

3. **Practice agape love.** What does *love* have to do with it? *Agape* is "unconditional love." It is expressed by individuals who offer respect, understanding, and compassion to all beings without hesitation, judgment, or conditions. Practicing this type of love without expectations or self-benefit is a wonderful way to practice abundance.

4. **Recognize that leadership has responsibilities and obligations.** To be a leader is not just about having followers. To be a leader places special obligations and responsibilities on those of us fortunate to carry this title. It means we are required to serve and help others in our charge, but also to operate through this lens in all areas of our lives. Truly effective leaders who embrace this definition of leadership operate out of abundance, not scarcity, and there is a ripple effect of positivity and goodness that emanates from their efforts.

One last concept my mother taught me during her long

life—and one I observe in other successful leaders who practice abundance—is to live life as a steward, not an owner. This is a simple yet profound belief, that we are the stewards of the gifts God has given us and not the owners of these gifts. To act with more abundance and be generous, we should acknowledge that we are not really the owners of anything we have in this world. We are meant to be stewards, and nothing we have been entrusted with truly belongs to us. If we operate as stewards and embrace the abundance mindset, we will find ample opportunities every single day to share these gifts even when life seems hard and we can't see beyond our own challenges.

Someone with an abundance mindset likely feels more positive, empowered, confident, and focused on serving others. They have opened themselves up to giving generously of themselves and their gifts. Someone with a scarcity mindset may feel overwhelmed, anxious, and frustrated with their life. They may find it difficult to share, give, or invest in others. We all have an option today to embrace abundance or scarcity as we interact with and lead those around us. Which will it be? And remember . . . always show up with a gift!

Reflect on the last thirty days. When have you exhibited either the abundance or scarcity mindset? Having read this chapter, how might you have shown up in a different way? Think about how you will utilize the tips in this chapter to embrace an abundance mindset more intentionally going forward.

CHAPTER 4

The Journey from Learning Jobs to Doing Work We Love

Every opportunity I got, I took it as a learning experience.
SATYA NADELLA, CHAIRMAN AND CEO OF MICROSOFT

I had a conversation with a young professional not long ago who was several months into his first post-college job. He was eager to grow his career and get started doing work he loves, but struggled to articulate what he thought success looked like or clearly define "work he loves." He described feeling bored, disengaged, and trapped in his current job and was thinking about starting a job search, even though he was working for a Fortune 500 company that recruited him out of college and was doing work directly related to his degree. When he expressed an interest in the work I do, this led to a discussion about the difference between *learning jobs* and *doing work we love.*

I shared my own professional journey with him, and he was surprised to hear about the eclectic path my career took over the years to help me learn what I was passionate about and how it prepared me engage in the work I do today. After graduating from college, I started out as a management trainee for a large retailer and learned how to run a business, engage with customers, and lead others as I progressed to more senior roles. I developed an interest in talent and recruiting while I was with the company and then transitioned to a large national restaurant chain, where I eventually became a senior executive leading recruiting, training, and diversity for the organization in my late twenties and early thirties. After four years, I was recruited to join and eventually lead a national executive search firm; there I developed a passion for coaching, leadership development, and writing. In my mid-forties, after a dozen years with this great firm, I decided to launch my own company so I could focus exclusively on the coaching and leadership development work I loved . . . and indulge my passion for writing. Along the way, I was blessed with great mentors and advocates who helped me and gave me wise counsel.

Why does all this matter? Each of the jobs I had until I started my own company was a *learning job*, and I am truly grateful for every growth opportunity, challenge, and lesson I experienced on the way to figuring out what I was passionate about and loved doing. The first twenty-five years of my career prepared me in multiple ways to better serve the clients I love working with today. As I shared with this young professional, how can we truly know what we love doing unless we experiment and explore different career experiences to see what fits? To be clear, I thoroughly enjoyed aspects of every work experience I had before I started my business. But, as time went on and I acquired new experiences, maturity, and hopefully a little wisdom, I began to better understand that I was being drawn to the work of coaching and guiding other leaders that I am so grateful to do today.

I could tell that our conversation was both enlightening and frustrating for this bright and talented future leader as he took it all in. He said he understood that it might take time, but still felt a degree of impatience that he might have to wait years to figure out what he loved to do. I gave him the following **six ideas** on how he might begin to both discern his calling and also maximize the learning experiences in his current job:

1. **Make a list of your skills.** What are you already good at? Also, what skills do you want to learn?
2. **Maximize your current role.** Are you pushing and stretching yourself? Are you fully executing your job and giving it 100 percent? Have you considered that doing well in the job you have versus chasing the job you don't have may be the wisest course of action?
3. **Ask your boss for help in creating a personal development plan.** Express your desire to grow and be intentional with your supervisor about discussing what you want to get out of your career. Get his or her input on what you can do to make this happen. How do you best utilize your skills and acquire new ones from your earlier list? Ask your supervisor and others to hold you accountable for making progress. Are there high-potential programs or other leadership development opportunities in your company you can be considered for when you qualify? Would outside leadership courses or an MBA be appropriate?
4. **Cultivate mentors and advocates.** Who do you admire in your professional and personal circles who can teach

you and help you grow? Who will give you candid feedback on how you are doing and what you need to work on? Who is willing to advocate for you and your career when you are not in the room? *Helpful Tip:* Mentor and advocate relationships are special and should be treated with professionalism and care. The people who agree to invest in you are giving generously of their time, and they should always feel your gratitude and appreciation.

5. **Always be willing to reflect in real time on your ongoing experiences and learnings.** Did you enjoy the project you just completed—and if so, why? What clicks with you? What excites you? What inspires you and makes you happy? As you gain more work experience, the picture of where you want to go will likely emerge and be clearer if you take the time to reflect on what is going around you, consider how it affects you, and savor what it is teaching you. Also, don't forget to consider how you are helping others and contributing to their success as part of your journey. I know without a doubt that this intentional reflection mindset helped me—and it's a lesson I learned from a wonderful mentor I had at my first job.

6. **Be patient and take stock at the end of every year.** You may not have to wait twenty-five years as I did to discern and engage in your dream work. At the end of every year, ask yourself if you have grown. What did you learn over the last twelve months? What new skills and experiences did you acquire? Are you challenged and learning new things? Did you get closer to understanding what you are

called to do? Is the dream job or work becoming clearer in your mind? Is it time to pursue it?

Finally, be open to the influence of life, love, faith, and family. As you carefully plan this exciting career journey, be mindful that life may throw you a few curveballs. For example, you may fall in love, get married, and have a family. In my experience, the adversities I have faced, my faith, my marriage, and my children have been crucial in shaping my journey to the fulfilling career I am blessed to enjoy.

My new acquaintance has plenty to think about, but I know he will find his way forward, and I plan to stay connected and help him any way I can. To his credit, he encouraged me to share the conversation that you have read about in this chapter. I have had plenty of *learning jobs*, and I am grateful for all the hard work I put in and every experience that shaped and prepared me for what I do today. Now, I embrace and live by the famous quote attributed to Mark Twain: "Find a job you enjoy doing, and you will never have to work a day in your life."

By the way, I may be doing work I love, but I still learn something new every day, and for that I am very grateful.

What has been your experience with learning jobs? Reflect on all of your work experiences and consider how they have shaped you into the professional you are today. Are you doing work you love? If not, how close are you to that goal? What new experiences do you need? What changes do you need to make to bring this to reality?

CHAPTER 5

Removing the Dead Trees in Our Lives

The world is indeed full of peril, and in it there are many dark places;
but still there is much that is fair, and though in all lands love is now
mingled with grief, it grows perhaps the greater.

J.R.R. TOLKIEN, *THE FELLOWSHIP OF THE RING*

In September 2020 we had three dead and dying trees removed from our yard, including a massive ash tree next to our house that caused my family much anxiety, worry, and stress during storms or windy days. Removing the trees was a complicated and expensive process due to their size and difficult access for the necessary machinery. When the trees were gone and new landscaping covered the scars of removal, we felt an immediate sense of relief and a feeling of peace for which we were all grateful. The entire process was cathartic in so many ways.

It dawned on me recently that in a sense, the removing of the dead trees from our yard is a clear metaphor for moving on past the challenges of the last few years to a better place. With the pandemic, civil unrest, economic upheaval, divisiveness, and political tension our nation experienced and is still experiencing, many of us are feeling stressed, anxious, burned out, and fearful of what the future holds. These are natural feelings, and you absolutely should not feel bad if you have them, but I hope we can agree that moving on to a better and more hopeful way of living is necessary and long overdue.

Perhaps we all have "dead trees" in our lives that need to be removed . . .

If you will indulge me, here are a few ideas and actions for embracing a way of living that might bring us all greater hope and peace of mind. If we continue with the dead tree metaphor, I believe that both "removing" and "replacing" are necessary.

- **Replace** the angst and fear that was so prevalent at the height of the COVID-19 pandemic by embracing a more hopeful post-pandemic future focused on better treatments and our ability to recover from COVID if we have it. We have to find a way to both live our lives and practice safety.
- **Remove** toxic influences in our lives, especially what we read online or watch on TV. Social media and news outlets obviously have their uses, but the daily deluge of bad news and negativity only leads to higher anxiety. Consider limiting or better filtering these bad influences in your life.
- **Replace** the isolation and loneliness we've experienced in the pandemic years with again meeting regularly with friends, family, work colleagues, and neighbors. Travel more if you can. Human beings must have community, and we paid a heavy price for living the virtual version of life we were forced to endure for so long. Working virtually

has been a surprisingly nice benefit for many of us, but don't let your home become a prison.

- **Remove** the excuses we tend to make about our health. Focus on self-care. Exercise. Eat better. Take care of your mental health. If you are working virtually or in a hybrid work environment, don't fill up the extra hours saved by less commuting with more work. Let's make an investment in ourselves.
- **Replace** worry about the future by doing something to make a positive difference in your circle of influence right now. Practice acts of kindness. Help others who are struggling. Donate time, talent, and treasure to great causes. "No one is useless in this world who lightens the burdens of another" (Charles Dickens).
- **Remove** the overreliance on our own strengths and abilities. It is absolutely OK to ask others for help. If faith is important to you, always trust in God and make time for prayer.

I removed three dead trees from my yard at the height of the pandemic and felt less anxiety, less stress, and an immediate sense of relief. I try very hard to practice the six ideas I have just shared, and by doing so I never fail to feel stronger and more hopeful. Perhaps this short chapter will prompt you to consider the "dead trees" that need to be removed and replaced in your life in the days, weeks, and months ahead. I sincerely hope so. Trust that better times are ahead!

In the coming week, reflect on what is creating anxiety and stress in your life. What could you possibly replace or remove in your life to feel more positive, energetic, and hopeful? Commit to making progress and share your efforts with a friend, work colleague, or family member to help hold yourself accountable.

CHAPTER 6

Reflecting on the Road
Less Traveled

The most difficult thing is the decision to act, the rest is merely tenacity. The fears are paper tigers. You can do anything you decide to do. You can act to change and control your life; and the procedure, the process is its own reward.

AMELIA EARHART

I recall a recent morning hike I took with my oldest son at a park near our home in the northern Atlanta suburbs. We came across a fork in the trail that made me think of Robert Frost's famous poem, *The Road Not Taken*,[1] and these lines in particular:

> Two roads diverged in a wood, and I—
> I took the one less traveled by,
> And that has made all the difference.

---

1 Robert Frost, *The Poetry of Robert Frost*, edited by Edward Connery Lathem (New York: Holt Rinehart and Winston, Inc., 1969).

Both this poem and that reflective day on the hiking trail stayed on my mind for weeks as I considered the choices and decisions I had made in my life and the ripple effect that followed. I have often taken the "less traveled path" and am grateful for the rich experiences, lessons learned, and the wonderful people I have encountered along the way. I haven't always made perfect choices, but by and large I feel a sense of contentment and appreciation for where my life is today. How often do you reflect on the decisions you have made and the paths you have followed in life?

As I consider these important experiences and decisions from my past, some were complete directional changes with my career, some involved embracing new ways of living, and some were profound mindset shifts. Reflecting on the process that led to embracing these choices, I remember leaning on the invaluable lessons I learned from my parents, the positive behaviors I observed from people I respect, my own intuition, and the values taught by my faith. Here are the **four insights** that stand out most:

1. **Understanding that my work exists to serve my family; my family does not exist to serve my work.** In chapter 1, I mentioned this profound shift in my thinking. In my early thirties, I was fortunate to enjoy a lot of career success, but my young family was making too many sacrifices due to my work travel, and I chose to make a fundamental shift in my thinking. I stopped asking my family to sacrifice for my work, and I began making career choices to better serve my family. Guess what? My career continued to thrive despite the

boundaries I placed around it and my decision to put my family first.

2. **Embracing a grateful mindset.** Long ago, my wife and I began working very hard to model a life focused on gratefulness for our sons and those we encounter each day, and we know this ongoing effort has absolutely transformed us. This also includes being grateful for our challenges and seeing the adversity we have endured in our lives as a blessing, not a burden.

3. **Living an authentic and integrated life.** I have worked very hard over the last twenty-plus years to be the same person in all areas of my life and strive to be consistently authentic as a businessperson, husband, father, community servant, and man of faith. I see all these disparate areas of my life as *integrated* and not existing in their own silos. I am very open about my life outside of work and am always interested in learning about others. Authenticity in today's world can be challenging, as we may fear judgment, isolation, or condemnation for expressing views out of sync with popular opinion, but I would argue that a life lived without authenticity is no way to live.

4. **Recognizing that our children are always watching us and will likely model later in life what they learn from our example.** When I was a young father, I got off the road and switched careers because my wife and I wanted our sons to grow up with our family having dinner together every night, and I wanted to follow the good example of being fully present for family set by my own parents. We pray together as a family every

night before we go to bed. As a family, we give our time, talent, and treasure to our church and community. We play games, we laugh, we listen to each other, we are honest with one another, and we make sure that love is present in our home. My wife and I do our best to model a good marriage for our sons. We are far from perfect, but we hope that by doing our best to model the right behaviors and live by the right values, they will do the same long after we are gone.

Many of us probably remember growing up thinking our lives would follow a certain path. As we grow older, we hopefully begin to recognize the overwhelming number of choices we can make every day about careers, relationships, where we live, how we live, etc. The surrounding culture and well-meaning people in our lives will always offer the paths they want us to follow. These paths will likely appear to be sensible, logical, offer worldly success, or anything else we may think we want out of life. I remember well the years when all I thought about was climbing the corporate ladder and earning a great living, because that was what everyone around me was doing.

Maybe you will make the relatively safe career and life choices that everyone else seems to be making, embrace conventional thinking, and be perfectly happy. But I would ask you to consider that the popular paths and the conventional choices may not be the best ones for you. Perhaps you should consider *the road less traveled* when you come to the fork in the road. Be willing to question "one size fits all" conventional wisdom. Trust your gut. Seek out wise counsel from the truth speakers in your life. Live by your values and follow your moral compass.

The easy and well-trodden path may not bring true fulfillment. It may not lead to truth or happiness. It may instead lead to an *ordinary* life when you were made for something *extraordinary*. Be willing to ask the tough questions and make the choices that work best for you and the kind of life you wish to live.

I spent plenty of time early in my career on the popular road. I was successful by the world's standard but *unfulfilled*. From my experience, the time I have spent on the road less traveled has often been difficult with lots of obstacles to overcome, but I am incredibly grateful for where my life is today and the opportunity I have to serve and help the people in my life. I wouldn't trade a minute of it. I chose to walk on the road less traveled, and that has made all the difference . . .

Over the next few days, reflect on at least two significant choices you have made in your life and consider if you made the right decision or wish you had made a different choice. Ponder why you feel that way. Do you have other imminent big decisions ahead of you? Will you take the safe path or consider the road less traveled?

CHAPTER 7

Generational Echoes

It is easier to build strong children than to repair broken men.
FREDERICK DOUGLAS

Our family enjoyed a weekend visit in the summer of 2021 from my then eighty-two-year-old father, Steve. During a quiet moment of conversation on our deck, my father and I talked about how much we both missed my mother, Sandi, who passed away in 2009 after a long illness. My parents were married for nearly half a century, a rare thing in today's world, and she was my father's best friend, partner, and wife as well as an inspiration to all who knew her. As we awkwardly spoke of our feelings of loss, the conversation eventually turned to a nostalgic recollection of her beautiful life. Old memories came flooding back for both of us, and I also learned valuable lessons as my dad shared experiences and insights into the multitude of tough decisions he and my mom had made over the years. I was very grateful in that moment to realize that my dad never missed an opportunity to share lessons that would help me to become a better father, husband, and me. They never stopped trying to teach me about life. I was blessed to have such a mother and am fortunate to have my father still with us.

I came to my senses in my mid-twenties, and the many seeds my parents planted in me began to take root. To paraphrase Mark Twain's famous quote, I was amazed at how smart my parents had become in the years since I had moved away from home! There were numerous stumbling blocks in front of me back then as I was building my career, but their words of wisdom kept coming back to me: "Do the right thing"; "Work hard and let your results speak for themselves"; "Treat others the way you want to be treated"; and "Put others before yourself." I find myself sharing these bits of wisdom with my own children, and I am grateful for the solid foundation my parents laid for me when I was growing up.

Do you ever stop and reflect on the lessons you learned in your childhood? Do you share those lessons with your children? If you plan to have children down the road, does this ever cross your mind? There is a vital need today for a return to the values of past generations. The "anything goes" mindset so pervasive in our culture today could benefit from clearer boundaries. Our children would only prosper if they could actually be children for a while and not be exposed to harmful influences at increasingly younger ages. Teaching our kids about faith, values, responsibility, manners, and the importance of a good work ethic is a critical responsibility for parents today. We desperately need to become more mindful of the surrogates who are attempting to raise our children without us and reassert our rights and responsibilities to be the primary influence while they still live in our home. Harken back to what I hope are positive memories of the lessons you learned from your parents and grandparents. Don't we have a responsibility to pass along all that is noble and worthwhile to our children?

As I was thinking about some helpful advice to offer working parents (and future parents) who read this chapter, I decided to not reinvent the wheel. The following is a list of **ten practical suggestions** that come from the important life lessons my parents passed along to me and my sister. I think we could all make a similar list from our collective past, and I hope you find this to be useful.

1. **Model** the right behaviors. Lead by example. Avoid "do as I say, not as I do!"
2. **Teach** the importance of faith, values, and the difference between right and wrong.
3. **Encourage** excellence and independent thinking.
4. **Listen** to your children's thoughts and ideas with patience and no judgment.
5. **Love** your children without reservation, but also love them enough to say no when necessary.
6. **Expose** them to God, nature, beauty, art, music, ideas, history, and different cultures.
7. **Invest** in quality family time and make it a priority.
8. **Instill** an appreciation for hard work and teach them how to be responsible with money.
9. **Create** boundaries and explain the rules. Discipline is important.
10. **Inspire** them to give back to the community and help others.

You may have a very different list, but these are some of the most impactful ways my parents taught me. My wife and I have worked hard to pass along the same lessons and others we believe are important to our children. Believe me, we have made a lot of mistakes along the way, but we try every day to do our best. It's a scary world out there, and I see a generation of children that are not being equipped to thrive in today's culture. If we don't accept full responsibility for raising and teaching our children, then someone or something will likely fill the void. That is the ugly reality.

I want to respectfully challenge you to do a few things. If your parents are alive, give them a call and reminisce a little about your childhood. Pick up an old photo album and be reminded of your youth and possibly better days. Look at your children when they are sleeping tonight and think about how you can prepare them for the real world. Ask yourself if they are on the path to be faith-filled, values-driven, hardworking, selfless people in a world that desperately needs these traits. Finally, ask yourself if one day they will hear the echoes of your positive influence on their lives . . . and pass on that priceless treasure to their own children.

Reflect on this chapter for a few minutes. If you are a parent, what are you doing to pass along "all that is noble and worthwhile" to your children? What grade would you give yourself? Where can you make improvements? If you are a future parent, what will you do now to prepare yourself for the wonderful responsibility of having children? How will you show up? How will you teach and guide them?

CHAPTER 8

Honoring the Impactful People in Our Lives

There is no greater joy nor greater reward than to make a fundamental difference in someone's life.

Sister Mary Rose McGeady, DC

On October 1, 2021, my older son Alex and I visited my dad in Florida on his eighty-third birthday and presented him with a very special gift. He knew I had written a new book, but he did not know it was dedicated to him and my mother. He learned about this surprise as he opened his present, a beautifully framed copy of the dedication page from my last book, *Essential Wisdom for Leaders of Every Generation*. My father is not a very emotional man, but this was a teary-eyed moment for him and for all of us who had gathered to celebrate his special day.

That book is dedicated to him and my dear departed mother because they both have been a source of so much wise counsel over the years. They were an inspiration to me and many others for the exemplary way they led their lives built around faith, family, generosity, and service to their community. I am so grateful that I had the opportunity to share this heartfelt moment of acknowledgment and gratitude with my father. I've done my best over the last several years to tell him how much he means to me and how grateful I am to be his son.

I wonder how often we miss opportunities to tell that select group of truly impactful friends, family, and work colleagues exactly how much they mean to us and the true difference they have made in our lives. We often wait until the end of a person's life to give a eulogy filled with nice things about someone and share how much they meant to us. *Why wait?* Why not say it now . . . when our words can have the most impact and they can hear from our lips the impact they made on us? *Why carry the burden of regret?* I experienced this profound regret myself as I gave the eulogy at my mother's funeral in 2009. Although I used this sorrowful occasion as an opportunity to honor her wonderful life, there is so much more I wish I had said to her during the years when she was still with us.

I encourage you to reflect on the people who have made a significant impact in your life. Think of those who have:

- Mentored you
- Encouraged you
- Inspired you
- Opened doors and created opportunities for you
- Given you wise counsel
- Loved you unconditionally for who you are
- Challenged you to do your best

- Been there for you when no one else was
- Told you the truth when nobody else had the courage

These teachers, coaches, mentors, former bosses, old college friends, and family members would likely love to know that what they said or did positively shaped the person you are today. I realize that my father will not always be with us, but I'm confident he will leave this earth knowing that he made a positive difference in the lives of the people he has encountered, that his family and friends love him, and that this world is a better place because of him. I believe my mother is looking down upon us from heaven and knows that her family and friends hold her in the same high regard.

The experience of writing *Essential Wisdom for Leaders of Every Generation* and honoring my parents made me more keenly aware of the people who need to hear from me more often, not just with a word of gratitude but with a deeper acknowledgment of the specific positive impact they have made (and are making) in my life. To be honest, I feel somewhat overwhelmed with the numerous opportunities to be more intentional in reaching out to the people who have helped me, inspired me, and taught me to better navigate the journey of life. As daunting as this task may be, I am determined going forward to stop feeling regret and let this treasured group of people from my past and present know the substantial impact they have had on me.

I keep thinking of Sister Mary Rose McGeady's quote at the beginning of this chapter. If, as she says, there is no greater joy or reward than to make a fundamental difference in someone's life, the responsibility to let those who have done this for us know the tremendous impact they have made in our lives falls squarely on our shoulders. I don't know about you, but I've got some work to do.

Reflect on who has positively impacted your life. How will you acknowledge their actions and honor them in the days ahead? How will you make this an intentional and consistent practice?

PART TWO

Practical Lessons for the Busy Leader

CHAPTER 9

Three Things Leaders Should Always Be Doing

Leadership is not about you; it's about investing in the growth of others.

KEN BLANCHARD

I often reflect on the countless conversations I have with leaders in my network and the consistent themes that are present in most of them. Many leaders are feeling challenged to varying degrees by open positions on their teams, retaining their people, economic challenges, and the ever-present stress of just doing their jobs and hitting the numbers. It can be easy and even understandable for leaders in such stressful times to just dig in and hold on . . . hoping to weather the storm.

I often share advice in my books and blog posts on practicing self-care, and I firmly believe all of us should be doing the best we can to take care of ourselves. But for those of us who are privileged to lead others, our teams and work colleagues need us to step up and do more. They need our help. The "Great Resignation" has multiple root causes, and among the various reasons people leave their jobs, we find COVID-19 burnout, dysfunctional or toxic organizations, lack of attention to the emotional and mental well-being of team members, lack of workplace flexibility, and poor management.

There is no easy answer to solve these challenges, but I have been recommending to leaders for years (even pre-COVID) a simple, three-step approach to engaging with their teams that is especially powerful and helpful in these difficult times: **Ask, Listen, and Invest**.

Ask the team. When you speak with your team members each week, consider sincerely asking these kinds of important questions (and welcome all responses):

- What are we doing right now that is working well?
- What do we need to do differently?
- What do I need to start, stop, or continue doing as your manager as we look at the year ahead of us?
- This is a stressful time for all of us, including me. How are you and your loved ones holding up?
- How can I better support and help you?
- What do you need most from me right now?
- What do you want out of your career? How can I best help you grow and develop?

Make sure to schedule frequent one-on-one conversations with team members and blend personal and business topics into the discussion. Consider being vulnerable with your team members about your own challenges, as it will most likely encourage them to be vulnerable with you in response to your questions. This cannot be a "check the box" exercise! Taking their emotional temperature and showing vulnerability and empathy must live alongside the routine business dialogue.

Note: Leaders have a responsibility to make sure the team feels "psychologically safe" to speak their minds. People need to be honest now (and always) without fear of negative repercussions, especially if they have the courage to offer a potentially great idea, point out a problem, or share their personal struggles. Also, give your team members sincere permission to be candid with you.

Listen to the team. OK, so you are asking the questions, but are you *really* listening? Good listening skills are a foundational strength of effective and successful leaders. Listen to difficult conversations and conflicting opinions with calmness, no judgment, and an open mind. We should consider responding with thoughtful follow-up questions to demonstrate we are really listening before offering our own opinions in return. If we are truly listening with a desire to learn and help, we must avoid defensiveness at all costs and even be willing to change our opinion if warranted. Also, it is absolutely OK to let team members vent and place their perception of the real issues on the table.

As you engage and listen to work colleagues during a challenge or crisis (or anytime for that matter), they need to first feel that they have a voice and are valued . . . and that as their leader you genuinely care about them and want to sincerely know what they think. The worst time to avoid engaging with team members is in the midst of difficult personal or professional periods in their lives. Nothing builds trust and deepens relationships more than allowing another person to feel listened to and valued.

Invest in the team. You have asked the right questions and actively listened. What's next? Consider how you will invest in the team this year and beyond. If you asked the right questions and listened well, you likely heard a number of ideas for helping team members feel more engaged, cared for, and appreciated. You heard what they need and want from you to help them grow their careers. All of us must be willing to make any necessary and reasonable tweaks within our power to give our teams what they need. How do we begin? Where do we start? There is much we can do right now to invest in our teams—here are **three examples**:

1. **Embrace flexibility with work arrangements.** Obviously, acceptance of virtual or hybrid approaches where possible is needed right now and is, in my opinion, an irreversible trend. After almost two years of the pandemic, we know we can still largely be effective without being in a corporate office behind a desk.

2. **Empower the team to get creative about boosting morale and overall engagement.** What are their great ideas? You don't have to think of everything yourself in a vacuum. Encourage them to help take ownership in this area and be willing to delegate to your team. From feedback I have heard from my clients, this effort has typically been a success.

3. **Invest in the team's growth and development.** How can you be a catalyst for elevating their skills, enhancing their work experiences, and encouraging overall career growth? Consider the weekly or bimonthly lunch-and-learn model where you share a helpful leadership article with the

team to discuss as a group or invite a guest speaker to speak on interesting topics. Some teams embrace the book club concept and read and discuss helpful books together. Ask your team what they wish to learn and get their help in designing a simple program. Investing in your team's development is a phenomenal retention tool!

We are in stressful times, and leaders are being sorely tested. We all hope the business and cultural swirl around us will slow down and something resembling normal will reemerge. As you take stock of what is going in your world as you read this book, consider that we who have the humbling privilege of being called leaders have an opportunity and responsibility to actively engage with our teams in the most helpful way possible. None of what I have shared is rocket science, but the key question is: *Are we actually doing it?*

One more thing . . . remember the old saying, "People leave managers, not companies"? It is hopefully a sobering thought that leaders and recruiters in other companies are calling your best people this week and asking the right questions, listening attentively, and promising to invest in them. The siren song of greener pastures is often difficult to ignore.

After reading this chapter, consider how you will be more intentional this week and beyond about asking, listening, and investing with your team. Have the courage to ask them for candid feedback on how you are doing in these three areas.

CHAPTER 10

How to Thwart Time Thieves (and Not Become One)

Time is the most valuable coin in your life. You and you alone will determine how that coin will be spent. Be careful that you do not let other people spend it for you.

CARL SANDBURG, PULITZER PRIZE-WINNING POET, BIOGRAPHER, AND JOURNALIST

Picture in your mind a likely familiar crime scene: the calendar. Every hour of every day during a typical business week, others (with likely good intentions) are trying to steal our time. "Time thieves" often hide right under our nose, comfortably situated between us and our work. The good news is that they leave clues at every crime scene. If we're going to improve efficiency, drive performance, and practice better self-care, we must expose the crimes that time thieves commit and make a serious effort to thwart them. We must also recognize and acknowledge that sometimes we are the time thieves, and our behavior may need to change as well.

What are some of the common ways others can steal our time?

- **Inviting us to unproductive or unnecessary meetings.** These are meetings that have no agenda, have no meaningful purpose, and don't really require our participation or are poorly run with no clarity of task ownership or accountability. A post by Zippia.com[2] on 2021 meeting statistics revealed that 71 percent of business meetings were deemed unproductive, and upper management spent over 50 percent of their time each week in meetings.
- **Forcing us to attend overly long meetings.** Often someone schedules an hour-long meeting when a ten-minute call or email exchange would have served the same purpose.
- **Failing to respect our time.** Others often forget to pause, for just a minute, and thoughtfully consider that every invitation extended to a colleague is an appropriation of their precious time. Is the meeting or call really worth asking for thirty minutes to an hour of our day?
- **Emailing, calling, or texting after hours and on weekends.** Nonemergency requests or information sharing steals personal time and is a failure to respect boundaries.

How do we identify and thwart our time thieves?

- **Conduct a calendar audit.** Print a copy of your calendar from a recent two-week period (and make this an intentional practice at least once a quarter). Make note of the meetings you attended where your presence was not really

---

2 Jack Flynn, "27 Incredible Meeting Statistics [2022]: Virtual, Zoom, In-Person Meetings and Productivity," https://www.zippia.com/advice/meeting-statistics/.

needed, the meetings that were poorly run with no agenda, or the meetings that could have been handled with a call or email. Make note of who invited you to these meetings. Who are the biggest repeat offenders?

- **Coach with respectful candor.** Respectfully and candidly address concerns with these repeat offenders. Ask probing questions about why they want us to attend their meetings. Discuss alternatives or suggest other members of the team. Offer suggestions for other ways to achieve their goals without scheduling a meeting. Respectfully share helpful ways they might make their meetings more effective. While trying to be helpful, be transparent about our desire to be more efficient with our time in order to focus on important work we are required to deliver.

- **Learn to say no.** Taking the bullet above one step further, we must learn to say no if we are to protect our time. We need to stop automatically saying yes to every calendar invitation, but the idea of saying no often fills us with dread. How will people react if we say no? The key is to say no to the time/meeting request, but still be helpful.

Here are **four helpful best practices** to effectively saying no:

1. Keep it simple, be honest, and keep emotion to a minimum. If we have a conflict, we should not give a rambling and ambiguous reason for our no, and we should not apologize or show excessive emotion. When we stumble over our response and show too much emotion, we convey that we are open to negotiation, which makes the discussion even more difficult. Also, trust that people can handle the real reason why we cannot attend. Try this: "Mike, I am not available to meet this afternoon as I have committed to attend my daughter's soccer game. Can we catch up tomorrow to discuss how the conversation with the team went?" Simple, honest, short, and unemotional.

2. Offer alternatives. I often say no, but I am always willing to offer alternatives if I think I need to attend the meeting or call. Try this: "Susan, 2:45 p.m. tomorrow doesn't work for me, but I am available at 4:00 p.m. Tuesday and 8:15 a.m. Wednesday. Which of those might work for you?" The "no" is clear, but alternatives are offered out of a desire to be helpful. In my experience, my audience almost always selects one of the alternative options.

3. Ask probing questions. One of the keys to saying no is to be curious and probe the reason for the request. What are the real needs of the other person? Consider asking:

- What are you trying to accomplish in the meeting/call?
- What do you need from me in the meeting/call?
- Do I have a clear role?
- Is there an agenda for the meeting?

Once you have gathered enough insight from your questions, you can then offer alternatives:

- "Bill, I think Gail's team addressed that last week in their meeting. I would connect with her before moving forward."
- "Thanks for explaining the purpose of the meeting. I actually think Kayla from my team is a better fit as she

is closer to the project. Please ask her to attend instead."

- "Craig, I understand there is no agenda for this meeting, and it sounds like a brainstorming session. I have a conflict, but I would be happy to do a quick call later this week to debrief, and perhaps I can attend a meeting with the group when you are further along."

4. Set after-hours boundaries. If we have colleagues or even bosses who email, call, or text us after normal business hours, we have four options:

- Say nothing and continue letting them steal our personal time.
- Turn off email notifications and silence our phones after hours so we will not be tempted to respond until normal business hours. Respectfully communicate that we are doing this to colleagues who have routinely reached out during these times.
- Go to the biggest offenders and a few key stakeholders. Respectfully ask them to respect our personal time. Let this select few have our home number to call if there is a true emergency.
- Be sure we model the right behavior and respect the personal time of our colleagues.

What are some of the ways we waste time, which is essentially stealing time from ourselves?

- **We overdo multitasking.** We are not actually being more efficient when we juggle ten things at once. We are likely doing ten things marginally well or even poorly which will require follow up, do-overs and ultimately waste more time. Instead, we can focus on doing fewer things at once and strive to give our full attention to (and complete) what is in front of us.

- **We don't protect our calendars.** We need to be more intentional about scheduling everything important on our calendars (professional and personal), including time needed to actually do our jobs and not let others steal it. A common complaint I hear from my network is the lack of time to get all of their work done during the day, which usually results in them doing it after hours.

- **We don't block out distractions.** I recently read that every time we are distracted by responding to an email or text, answering calls, or looking at social media while in the middle of other important work, it takes a whopping twenty-three minutes and fifteen seconds to get refocused on what we were doing. What a time waster! We have to show more self-discipline and give ourselves distraction-free time each day for important work. A best practice is to only check and respond to emails and phone messages at set times during the working day. I recommend early morning, just after lunch, and late afternoon. We live in a world where an instant reply is expected, but is it really necessary? Turning off email notifications and silencing the phone are great places to start addressing the issue.

- **We struggle with prioritization.** In today's hectic world, we tend to treat everything as urgent instead of focusing on our key priorities. My Leadership Foundry co-founder Brandon Smith has written extensively about the dangers of treating everything as urgent and the importance of prioritization. If everything is urgent, then nothing is urgent. He reminds us that prioritizing well requires intentionality, self-discipline, and a focused use of resources and patience.

- **We don't manage our energy well.** If most of us begin the day with a full battery, depending on our personality types and work styles, we may lose energy from that battery throughout the day. When we fail to practice adequate self-care and replenish the battery or work around low-energy periods, we can be less efficient in our use of time. How do we schedule and integrate activities into our daily calendars that give us energy? Can we fit in some exercise during the day? Schedule alone time if we are introverts? Schedule more face time with the team if we are extroverts? Schedule all of our administrative tasks at the end of the day when our energy is likely at a low point?
- **We don't delegate.** We waste time when we consistently fail to delegate. As leaders, delegation is an excellent way to develop team members and help them grow. If we are stuck in the weeds and focused on minutiae, we are potentially wasting valuable hours that could be invested in developing those around us, strategizing, brainstorming, and other forward-looking leadership activities.

Time thieves are everywhere, and in most cases, they may not be aware they are stealing our time away. The best practices and insights I've shared here will help us identify and coach them to stop. We have to set appropriate boundaries, clearly communicate our expectations, and be more intentional if we want to turn the calendar from a crime scene into an effective and efficient example of time well spent. We also need to be mindful of the six ways we waste our own time and do our best to shed or avoid those bad habits.

Let's be honest. You and I may, at times, be the time thieves I've identified in this chapter. Not sure? After reading these insights, reflect on last week at work. Honestly ask yourself if you wasted the time of your colleagues in any of the ways I mentioned. Ask your colleagues for candid feedback if you have committed the crime of time theft. It's not too late to change these bad habits as well.

After reading this chapter, conduct a calendar audit as recommended. Who are your time thieves? Using this chapter's best practices as a guide, map out a personal action plan to push back and start reclaiming precious time to apply in other critical areas. After thirty days of using your plan, do another audit to determine how much time you have reclaimed each week.

CHAPTER 11

Are You Working in a Dysfunctional Meeting Culture?

Even if people had nothing else to do with their time, the monotony of sitting through an uninspired staff meeting, conference call, or two-day off-site would have to rank right up there with the most painful activities of modern business culture. And when we consider that most of the people struggling through those meetings do indeed have other things to do, that pain is only amplified.

PATRICK LENCIONI, *DEATH BY MEETING*

Before you read the rest of this chapter, I would like you to engage in a brief reflection exercise. Close your eyes and think about where you spent your time over the last two weeks at work. How much of your time was spent in meetings? How many of the meetings were productive with clear agendas, specific actions assigned to participants, and defined deadlines for those action items? How many meetings, *upon reflection*, were repetitive, had no agendas, did not really require your presence, or could have been handled by an email or brief conference call? Did you have enough time over the last two weeks to actually do all the work your job requires during the workday—or did it spill over into your personal time?

What were the results of your reflection exercise? Any epiphanies? How is this affecting your morale? The vast majority of professionals I engage with have a high degree of frustration with the structure, volume, and even the necessity of many of the meetings they are forced to attend each week. They will often acknowledge that they may be contributing to the problem themselves with how they conduct meetings they are responsible for leading. I have written extensively in my book *Essential Wisdom* on best practices for fixing dysfunctional business meetings and better time management, and we covered thwarting time thieves in chapter 10 of this book. All of this content can help you effectively improve how you spend your time and structure, lead, and participate in meetings, but I would like to elevate awareness in this chapter about why we have such widespread challenges with meetings.

Normalized Defects and Accidental Values

As you will read in chapter 17 of this book, I write about the "normalization of defects" in business. I learned from my friend and fellow author Steve Moore about NASA's uncovering of the imbedded defects, known by many, in the space shuttle program that led to the tragic Columbia and Challenger shuttle explosions. *Normalized defects* can be defined as those behaviors and actions we do and tolerate, even though we likely know at some level they are wrong. Steve has done a wonderful job of applying this concept to the business world in some of his leadership consulting work. In business, you often hear this described as "That's just the way we do things around here," and these defects can become embedded in a team or company culture over time. Let's consider our challenges with meetings through the prism of *normalized defects*: We likely know we have a big issue with unproductive meetings, but we have gotten used to it over time and may not know how to change. We may even fear changing because we have gotten so used to the widespread "meeting culture" we have created and may be skeptical of more effective and efficient approaches. Broadly acknowledging at all levels of an organization the widespread nature of a normalized defect like dysfunctional and unnecessary meetings (and committing to substantive change) can be a significant step forward in fixing the problem.

I came across a post on HBR.com by bestselling author Patrick Lencioni several years ago where he discussed the various types of values in an organization. I was particularly drawn to his description of *accidental values*:

> *Accidental values* arise spontaneously without being cultivated by leadership and take hold over time. They usually reflect the common interests or personalities of the organization's employees. Accidental values can be good for a company, such as when they create an atmosphere of inclusivity. But they can also be negative forces, foreclosing new opportunities. Managers always need to distinguish core values from merely accidental ones, as confusion here can be disastrous.[3]

He also wrote about connecting your core company values to how and where you spend your time each day. It would

---

3 Patrick Lencioni, "Make Your Values Mean Something," https://hbr.org/2002/07/make-your-values-mean-something.

seem logical that we would spend the majority of our time on activities that reflect our company values, correct? As I shared in chapter 10, a recent extensive survey of meetings and their impact on where we spend our time determined that 71 percent of business meetings were deemed unproductive and upper management spent over 50 percent of their time each week in meetings.

The survey also went into great detail about the millions of work hours lost to unproductive meetings and the billions of dollars lost each year on them (two of the many financial reasons why we should take on the meeting dilemma without delay). This could lead us to conclude, perhaps, that meetings have become an *accidental value* in many companies based on this exorbitant time investment. I know leaders right now who would say they are in meetings 70 to 90 percent of their time each week. Do we really want to communicate internally to our employees or externally to our customers and clients that *meetings* have become a value of our company? Of course not . . . but the problem still remains.

What Can We Do?

There are countless books and articles on best practices for improving meetings or implementing better alternatives. There is value in learning these approaches, and I encourage you to pick up my last book or read my blog posts if you would like to dive deeper. My challenge to leaders and aspiring leaders who read this post is to start having respectfully candid conversations in your companies at all leadership levels on this topic. Challenge the status quo and look at root causes for your meeting issues. Ask probing questions:

- Are our meetings effective and efficient?
- Are there better alternatives such as email, easily accessible dashboards for status updates, or brief conference calls?
- Why do we have so *many* meetings?
- Do we have adequate time to do our work and if not, are our teams taking work home?
- Is there a good reason why we treat some meetings as sacred?
- Can we embrace the popular trend of one or two meeting-free days during the week?
- What are we neglecting or ignoring regarding the business and our people by spending time in unproductive meetings?

Although I am a firm believer in the positive ripple effect one leader or team can have on others in an organization when they model changing attitudes, helpful behaviors, and new tactics, I think fixing meeting madness requires a more systemic approach. Treat it as a cultural issue (which it is) and meet it head on from the top of the organization down. Be willing to question the causes of the disease and come up with large-scale cures before putting additional energy into addressing the symptoms.

A Much-Needed Outcome

I was chatting with a senior HR executive client not long ago and mentioned the topic of this chapter to her. She reminded me of the obvious and much-needed outcome we will have if we succeed in fixing the dysfunctional meeting culture that exists in most companies: *We will have more time for the meetings that matter most with our colleagues and team members.* Leaders consistently share with me that they have not been spending enough quality one-on-one time with their peers or the members of their teams. The pandemic had an obvious negative impact, but as we move into a post-pandemic phase we can (and must) begin improving relationships strained by two-plus years of remote work. It's time to invest in improving teamwork and trust with our colleagues. We can be committed to developing our people and seeking developmental conversations to assist our own growth and development. If you could reclaim five to ten hours of your week by addressing the challenges of your company's meeting culture, how would you invest this gift of time?

Meetings are obviously a necessary part of business, and I am certainly not advocating for their complete elimination. But I hope you will agree that we can do better and make significant improvements. Some meetings are just unnecessary. Some are poorly run and can be improved. Some can be replaced by more effective and less time-consuming alternatives. Senior leaders need to recognize the systemic challenges and advocate for big changes. I hope this chapter stimulates some new thinking and inspires you to engage in a different conversation about meetings in your company. The applause will be deafening if you get it right.

Take a few minutes and reflect on the content in this chapter. Do you work in a dysfunctional meeting culture? Are you willing to engage in positive actions to influence change? Begin by examining over the next few days how you lead meetings . . . and the necessity of the ones you host. Where can you make changes? Begin asking your colleagues the probing questions I shared and engage in positive discussions to help others rethink meetings within your sphere of influence.

CHAPTER 12

The Power of Self-Discipline, Intentionality, and Routine

The key is not to prioritize your schedule
but to schedule your priorities.

Stephen R. Covey

Many of us wrestle at the end of each year over which priorities to concentrate our attention on after January 1st. I wonder if our priority lists actually vary much from year to year or if they typically include a vague focus on health goals, family time, time with friends, acquiring new skills, business success, personal financial goals, etc. Perhaps we will get very specific in the form of resolutions about certain things we will do or bad habits we will drop. I would suggest that a better use of our time is considering how to improve our self-discipline and embrace intentionality versus narrowly focusing on which priorities make the list. We likely know what we need and want to do, but we may struggle to get it all done. Perhaps one of the best places to start is considering where we spend our time and developing useful routines. Let me give you an example.

For many years, I have been intentional about finding time for and preparing at the beginning of each day to be at the top of my game for clients, friends, and family. I have been an early riser since childhood, and my early morning ritual has been consistent for the last few decades. While some people like to exercise early in the day, I prefer to work out at lunch or late in the afternoon as a form of stress release and use my early morning time for prayer, deep thinking, reading, and creative writing. I wake up at 4:45 a.m. every day and enjoy the first of my two cups of coffee. I say a prayer and do some spiritual or business reading, always looking to feed and expand my mind. I have a healthy breakfast, enjoy a second cup of coffee and do some writing, usually a blog post or a chapter for a future book. I sometimes work on creating new leadership development content for my business. Around 6:15 a.m., I check on the news of the day, send a few emails, manage administrative aspects of my business, and prepare for my first meeting, which is typically at 7:00 or 7:30 a.m. Monday through Friday. I follow a similar routine on the weekends— without the early meetings and emails, of course.

This focused routine prepares me to fully engage with the leaders I work with and be an alert and active listener/coach attuned to their needs. I feel sharp, creative, and focused, and I credit this intentional and disciplined approach to starting the day for allowing me to give the best of myself to others. I am grateful that my business has thrived over the years, in part because of this morning ritual and its impact on my day. Note: I followed this same routine pre-COVID, but typically left my home by 6:45 or 7:00 a.m. each weekday to drive to my first coffee meeting of the day.

Two of the keys to improving self-discipline, mastering intentionality, and developing routines are *practicing self-awareness* and *learning how to say no*. For example, I have known most of my life that I am naturally sharpest and have the most energy in the morning. As a high-functioning introvert, I also know I will be at my best engaging with others from 7:00 a.m. to around 4:00 p.m. most days. I am typically scheduled with individual clients or leadership teams the vast majority of each day Monday through Friday.

Because high-functioning introverts tend to run out of energy for people by mid to late afternoon, I carve out thirty to forty minutes for exercise (usually intense cardio) between 11:00 a.m. and 1:00 p.m. every day, and I also take a two-mile walk at the end of the workday (weather permitting) before family dinner. These exercise windows allow me to relieve stress, partially restore my energy for people, and contribute significantly to my overall mental health and physical fitness.

The end of the day walk is particularly important to me as I turn my phone off, pray a Rosary, and use the remaining walking time for deep thinking and reflection. I am then ready to fully engage with my family at dinner and be present for them the rest of the evening.

I am self-aware about my needs, but I have also worked hard for years at learning to effectively say no. The exercise time on my calendar is the time slot I work hardest to protect. It has been a fixture on my calendar since early 2020, and I schedule all of my work around it. There are a few exceptions when I will move the exercise time, but they are rare. When I say no to someone who wants this protected time slot, I offer alternative times and do my best to be helpful and accommodate their request when it will work for both our calendars.

Why does all this matter?

The leaders I admire and try to emulate wisely practice self-care and are intentional about taking care of their physical, emotional, spiritual, and mental needs. They understand (and I completely agree) that you cannot share with others from an empty cup.

One last helpful tip to promote better self-discipline, intentionality, and useful routines is to place every important personal and professional goal or to-do on the calendar each week. This may seem obvious, but in my experience most businesspeople only schedule the work-related items and fail to schedule the equally or more important personal stuff. The result is that the priorities and important areas of our personal lives only get the scraps of time left over from our hectic workdays. Be more intentional. Schedule everything important in your life (kid's activities, exercise, doctor visits, thinking time, prayer time, volunteering, anniversaries, birthdays, etc.) to ensure that nothing falls through the cracks. In my life, if something is on my calendar, it is highly likely to get done.

Working and living in the age of COVID has affected all of us for better or worse. Although I greatly respect the severity of the pandemic and its impact on people's lives, I also am grateful for the forced positive changes in work habits and routines many of us have experienced. In the old days, I left my home early to meet with clients throughout the day and got home just in time for dinner. Today, I feel very fortunate to run my business with a hybrid approach that allows me to work virtually and schedule in-person meetings more selectively, which is currently about four to five times per week. My business is thriving, I feel healthy and fully engaged, my productivity is vastly improved, and my clients are well-served. I believe the hybrid work model is here to stay, and I embrace it.

I don't pretend to have all the answers, and I often struggle to do all of this well like most businesspeople I know, but I keep trying to improve. Time is a precious resource, and we need to be good stewards of how we spend it. I believe greater intentionality, good routines, and better self-discipline are the keys to igniting more success in life and business. If we achieve progress in making this a reality, life and work will be richer and more enjoyable because of our efforts.

After reading this chapter, how will you think differently about work and life this week and beyond? What steps can you begin making to develop better self-discipline, be intentional, and adopt healthy routines? How can you reinforce what is already working for you?

Helpful Tip: *Find an accountability partner so you can challenge each other to make improvements, then frequently share your progress with them.*

CHAPTER 13

Avoiding the Workaround Traps

*In any moment of decision, the best thing you can do is
the right thing, the next best thing is the wrong thing, and
the worst thing you can do is nothing.*

THEODORE ROOSEVELT

I think we can all agree that the most direct path between points
A and B on a graph is a straight line. I hope we can also agree that
most of us would prefer to be as productive, efficient, and effective
as possible in our daily work. This is obvious, right? But, in my
experience, I often see leaders and teams avoid taking the most
helpful and direct path when it comes to making decisions, being
productive, and addressing challenges by engaging in an ongoing
series of "workarounds" to get things done. Webster's Dictionary
defines *workaround* as "a plan or method to circumvent a
problem without eliminating it." This is a common business trap
that overcomplicates decision making, slows down execution,
contributes to burnout, and wastes precious time. Have you ever
fallen into the "workaround trap"?

I shared the idea for this chapter with a senior executive in my circle, and it was interesting to see his surprised reaction when, after a moment of self-reflection, he realized how often he succumbs to this common trap. We unpacked a number of his work experiences that closely resembled similar situations causing workarounds in other organizations that I have observed over the years. He began to understand that rather than directly addressing the issues that were uncomfortable to acknowledge or lurking just below the surface, he and his colleagues had developed overly complicated approaches and responses that were impeding their success. In the case of his company's longstanding and unproductive approach to business meetings, he realized that he had chosen to just accept this as "the way we do things around here." Do any of the situations below sound familiar?

- Teams are required to attend multiple unproductive, poorly planned, and time-wasting meetings to address and rehash the same business issues, with little progress being made.
- Two teams are tasked with collaborating to develop a new solution for a customer, but the outcome is insufficiently defined, communication is poor, and decision-making rights are not clear. Out of frustration, the teams retreat back into their silos and develop competing solutions rather than collaborate to create one together.
- A leader avoids assigning important tasks or projects to a team member who is struggling and not performing well, but the leader won't directly address the performance issues.
- Instead of speaking up in a meeting and saying the difficult

things required to help the team make the right decision, team members engage in unproductive sidebar discussions with colleagues after the meeting to say what they really think.

- A leader asks multiple team members to work on a project or initiative without clear role clarity and ownership out of a desire to avoid the potential conflict of selecting just one leader to be in charge.
- Team members routinely multitask during meetings. They check email and do other work because they are in so many meetings each day . . . and don't have time to do their jobs.
- Unclear direction on a strategy or important initiative is given and team members are unsure what to do, so they engage in unproductive "guessing" about what is required instead of challenging the boss and clarifying what is being asked of them.

These are some of the numerous (and very real) scenarios that often lead us to unproductively work around the challenges we may face each day at work instead of addressing them head on. The real danger of the workaround trap is how subtly it can sneak up on us and become a normal (and accepted) way of doing business.

Focusing on the Three C's

What are some common causes for this trap and what can we do to avoid falling into it? This is not the definitive list, but I would suggest that leaders can avoid or reduce workaround traps like the ones I shared earlier by focusing on improvement in **three key areas**:

1. **Candor**. Are we being honest, open, and direct with our colleagues? Have we done our part to make it psychologically safe for our colleagues to speak with candor in public settings? Are we willing to identify the "elephant in the room"? When we fail to actively embrace candor at work, it can contribute to distrust, politics, stifled innovation, slower decision making, inefficiency, and poor execution. Our willingness to consistently engage in respectfully candid dialogue will decrease these negative outcomes and reduce the need for workarounds to solve challenges we should be addressing and solving at the onset.

2. **Clarity**. Consider how often we waste precious time, create inefficiencies, and hamper execution because of a lack of clarity. When we don't clearly answer the why, who, what and when questions at the beginning of a project, during a business meeting, or in any communication we share with our team members, we contribute to uncertainty and confusion. If we combine a lack of clarity with a culture that doesn't embrace candor, leaders and team members will likely not push back and ask for the clear direction and answers they need to be successful.

3. **Calendar**. Let's be honest: business meetings are sometimes worshipped as a sacred cow that nobody has the courage to oppose. Many companies today endure the triple whammy of meetings that are too frequent, poorly timed, and badly run. This leads to losses in productivity, poor collaboration, and negative impacts on the well-being of both teams and individuals. This greatly contributes to the challenge of workarounds when we are scrambling

to find time to do the actual work associated with our jobs. What if you had more time to think, reflect and plan? What if you could focus and reduce distractions? Take control of the calendar. Be more discerning about which meetings you attend. Learn to say no when necessary rather than agreeing to every meeting request. Block out meeting-free periods on your calendar so you have time for your own work. Identify and thwart the time thieves in your life as you learned about in chapter 10.

I encourage the readers of this chapter to look in the mirror and do a little self-reflection as my senior executive friend did during our conversation. Have you or your colleagues been falling into workaround traps? Are you looking to increase productivity, improve efficiency, and be more effective? Consider doing a quick audit of what you and your team have been working on this year and determine if workarounds exist. If they do, apply the Three C's litmus test and see if improving in these three areas can eliminate or improve the issue(s). I'm confident you will see an immediate and positive difference.

Remember, the most direct path between points A and B is a straight line.

Before moving on to the next chapter, consider if you have fallen into any workaround traps over the last thirty days. What were the key reasons? Try the ideas shared in this chapter to extract yourself from the traps and avoid them in the future.

CHAPTER 14

What Can a Twelfth-Century Saint Teach Modern Leaders about Candor?

Nothing in the world is harder than candor,
and nothing is easier than flattery.

FYODOR DOSTOYEVSKY

You may recall reading about St. Thomas Becket in your history classes years ago. He was Archbishop of Canterbury from 1162 until his murder in 1170 and is venerated as a saint and martyr by the Catholic Church. He engaged in conflict with Henry II of England over the rights and privileges of the Church and was murdered by followers of the king in Canterbury Cathedral. Soon after his death, he was canonized a saint by Pope Alexander III. There is much we can learn from the courageous defense of truth and justice that cost St. Thomas Becket his life. But there is something else of significance that this saint from the twelfth century can teach us—especially those of us in business leadership roles. Reflect on these words of St. Thomas Becket to a friend on the way to his ordination as Archbishop of Canterbury:

> Hereafter, I want you to tell me, candidly and in secret, what people are saying about me. And if you see anything in me that you regard as a fault, feel free to tell me in private. For from now on, people will talk about me, but not to me. It is dangerous for men in power if no one dares to tell them when they go wrong.

I am drawn to the last sentence in particular: "It is dangerous for men in power if no one dares tell them when they go wrong." Over the course of my thirty-plus years in business, I have noticed the consistent frequency with which business leaders lose the candid voices in their lives as they climb the corporate ladder. It is a common scenario for these professionals to reach a senior leadership position where people who were once peers and co-workers become followers. They find it difficult to receive honest feedback, and open dialogue with their team is rare. To make matters worse, bad news is often diluted or kept from them. These leaders understandably get frustrated when very little changes after they repeatedly ask for candor and begin to recognize that they are, to some degree, flying blind without a reliable compass. Lack of candor on a team or in the larger corporate culture also stifles productivity and innovation, ultimately having a negative impact on business results. What can these leaders do? Does this describe you or someone you know?

On the Inside

It is very difficult to change human nature. You may never

fully overcome the fear, politics, and self-protective behaviors exhibited by the rank and file in your organization, but the effort must be made. Leaders should always work diligently to build trust and create opportunities for safe and open dialogue with their team members. First, let's consider an "inside the company" approach. Here are **five suggestions**:

1. **Teach.** Teach the team what you are seeking and appropriate ways to share it; most importantly, tell them *why*. Newer generations entering the workplace in particular will want to understand the reason. Also, make it clear that you won't shoot the messenger . . . and really mean it!

2. **Model.** It is imperative that leaders model the desired behavior. A starting point might be to bring up difficult issues in meetings, even if they reflect poorly on you, and deal with them openly in front of the team.

3. **Praise.** When you do observe sincere efforts to share ideas and honest feedback, praise this behavior in front of the rest of the team. Do it frequently, consistently, and in public.

4. **Ask the New Folks.** If you want a refreshing viewpoint of what is going on in your organization, seek the opinions of employees who have been there less than three months. Engage in low-profile discussions away from the spotlight with new hires—you will be amazed at what you will learn.

5. **Restrain Your Ego.** All of the above may sting a bit if you have been surrounded by the "yes" crowd and are not used to criticism and honest feedback, as much as you desire it. Remember that humility and vulnerability

are the hallmarks of good leadership. These actions will help you grow as a leader (and deepen the engagement and commitment level of your team) if you are sincere.

St. Thomas Becket realized the dangers of living in isolation and implored a friend to be a candid voice in his new role as a powerful archbishop. Business leaders should follow a similar path. Have enough humility and self-awareness to realize you will make mistakes and don't have all the answers. Invest in your own personal growth and don't become complacent, surrounded by people who agree with everything you say and refuse to challenge you to become better at your job.

Looking Outside

Where else can you find the necessary candid voices? Outside of your company are numerous professionals with talent and great ideas that can help you grow, if you know how to find them. You have at least **three viable options** to consider:

1. **Seek out a mentor.** Seek a senior executive from another organization who has successfully done what you are hoping to do with your career, has had experiences you wish to learn from, or possesses values you admire. (I suggest getting referrals from people you trust to help in finding the right person.) After you get to know the person and go through your own vetting process, humbly ask them if they will consider being your mentor. Finding the right person can take a while, but the journey is worth it. I have had several mentors in my career and the experiences were invaluable. Don't be surprised

by what you can learn from someone who takes seriously the role of mentor. This is only effective if you are willing to humbly listen and follow their helpful advice.

2. **Enlist a personal board of advisors.** Go to business leaders you know and trust in different companies and ask them to be part of your inner circle of advisors. This isn't necessarily a formal meeting, but a small group of people who have nothing to lose by being absolutely candid and objective with you. View them as your accountability partners, which is completely different from a mentor relationship. Don't select close friends for this group who may be reluctant to say the difficult things, but instead seek people who will challenge you.

3. **Find an executive coach.** This person should be objective, direct, and not limited by the challenges internal employees of your company face in being honest. Interview a number of coaches, check references, and select one who can be your candid counselor and help you stay on the right path. Great coaches will always tell you the truth, even when it is painful.

St. Thomas Beckett had it right and knew he needed candid voices in his new and powerful role. Don't be lulled into an unfounded self-confidence because you only hear positive feedback from those around you. Also, remember that the absence of feedback from your team does not constitute a positive endorsement of your work. My most successful executive coaching clients utilize most of the options I have laid out in this chapter. Despite their positive business results, they always assume there is room for improvement and actively seek honest feedback to help them grow and stay on track. Who are the candid voices in *your* life?

Take some time to truly ponder this idea of candor. Do people tell you the difficult things? Do you get honest and candid feedback from key stakeholders and team members around you? Using the ideas in the chapter, engage in a sincere effort in the coming weeks to grow the candid voices in your life—you will not regret it.

CHAPTER 15

How to Avoid Becoming an Unconnected Leader

Networking is a lot like nutrition and fitness: We know what to do, the hard part is making it a top priority.

Herminia Ibarra, PhD, professor at London Business School

As they ascend the corporate ladder, many leaders do a curious thing: They stop networking and don't seem as interested in growing new professional relationships. This can have a significant long-term negative impact on a career in a number of ways. I have observed this phenomenon over much of my professional life, most recently in conversations with a number of senior business leaders who have unexpectedly found themselves in career transition or are considering looking for new roles. Many spend the first few months of the job search rebuilding networks they failed to maintain while employed. However, the need for leaders to maintain effective, dynamic networks goes well beyond a possible date with destiny in the ranks of the unemployed.

In spite of our hectic schedules, networking and relationship building is essential to forward-looking leadership. Leaders with strong networking skills benefit themselves, their organizations, their community, and the people in their network. Networking is more than creating a safety net for an inevitable period of career transition; it is a means to access an enormous pool of resources with unlimited benefits. The reasons executives stop networking are manifold, and I will address many of them in this chapter. More importantly, I will speak to the investment required and the payoff for those who do it well.

The Obstacles

Why is networking a challenge for many leaders today? What gets in the way? There are **six fundamental obstacles** that I hear on a consistent basis:

1. **"I don't have enough time to network."** This is the easiest to overcome, as you will see in the investment section of the article. This is simply a scheduling and commitment issue.
2. **"I am doing just fine and don't need any help."** For years I have observed that leaders often fall into the "complacency trap" and fail to see the benefits of engaging with new people and being exposed to different ideas and new ways of thinking.
3. **"My job is secure, so I don't need to spend time meeting new people."** Unfortunately, I have seen too many leaders who felt safe in their positions fall victim to corporate downsizing. This false sense of job security was once rampant, but the reality of fading company loyalty in today's economy is finally taking hold.

4. **"I'm on LinkedIn, so I am networking."** This helpful tool serves a useful purpose and can absolutely enhance networking, but it should not replace the face-to-face human interaction required in effective network building.

5. **"I'm not very good at making new connections and, in fact, find it intimidating."** This is a common admission for many. Remember that networking can and should be tailored to your style and personality. The secret is to find the method that maximizes your strengths, regardless whether you are an introvert or an extrovert.

6. **"I didn't do any substantive networking during the forced isolation of COVID, and I am struggling to figure out how to do this in the post-pandemic era."** This is a legitimate concern, but it can also be a crutch. Networking and meeting new connections can just as easily occur virtually, and professionals are learning to adapt to this approach, which we will unpack later in the chapter.

Helpful Tip: I find the best way to encourage a shift in thinking is to ask challenging questions (of myself or others):

- Does my team have the best talent available?
- Am I getting the personal development I need?
- Is my job secure and if not, do I have a network of people who can help me?
- Do I have quick access to helpful professional resources and competitive intelligence outside my company?
- Do I wield the appropriate level of influence in my organization?

- Do I have all of the meaningful business relationships I will ever need?

If you answered "no" to any of these questions, this chapter was written for you.

The Investment

OK, you understand the importance of networking and its potential obstacles, so what comes next? Networking must be a priority. Rethink your calendar. Make in-person interaction the ultimate goal versus simply connecting virtually, but virtual calls are an acceptable substitute depending on geography and overall convenience. Vibrant networks take time to build and a long-term commitment to sustain and grow them. Here are **five practical ways** to make a meaningful investment in networking:

1. **Take an honest look at your calendar.** If you see little time for networking, let me challenge you a bit. There are five opportunities a week for coffee and/or breakfast and five opportunities a week for lunch. Start utilizing at least one of these times each week to meet with someone new (or nurture an existing work relationship). You have to eat, so why not spend this time with another professional and accomplish two objectives? You can also enjoy coffee virtually with a new or existing connection, which became very popular during the recent pandemic.

2. **Make time to nurture relationships in your network, both in and out of your organization.** Nurture these relationships at the same time you are expanding new

ones. Relationships must be maintained, and this takes work. The worst thing you can do is reach out to someone in your hour of need and realize that you failed to maintain the relationship.

3. **LinkedIn is my recommended tool for connecting through social networks.** It is important to have a complete and robust profile detailing your professional and academic background along with a professional picture. I encourage you to read the countless posts available online to help you develop your own strategy and make the best use of LinkedIn. As I mentioned in the Obstacles section, LinkedIn is a valuable tool, and it can help you identify and contact other helpful professionals as long as you also commit to making a personal connection as well.

4. **Attend or host relevant speaker events, workshops, seminars, or other social mixers to meet fellow professionals.** Keep an eye out for relevant speaker events and make an effort to attend in-person or virtually when possible. Consider hosting or co-hosting events virtually, either at your office or another venue. Organizing breakfast or lunch meetings with notable speakers on relevant topics allows you to play host and invite other business leaders you might not meet with other approaches. I have hosted speaker events for over twenty years, and this is an excellent way to connect with other professionals.

5. **Volunteer and get involved in the community.** Where is your passion? What causes excite you? Getting involved, first and foremost, should be about helping

others. But volunteering your time and serving on non-profit boards are excellent ways to meet like-minded professionals. Jo Ann Herold, author, coach and experienced chief marketing officer, shared this insight with me one morning over coffee:

> Networking and volunteering have always been important in my career. I like to join organizations I am passionate about and I abide by the old saying: The more you give, the more you receive! I try to take a leadership role when I volunteer because it's a great way to get to know the organization, the members and the people we serve.

Helpful Tip: Integrate networking into other activities. Neighborhood swim meets, kid's sports' practices, and community volunteering all can be fortuitous opportunities to meet other professionals. I have found more success in these casual settings than through any other avenue. There is something authentic about connecting initially as parents or like-minded businesspeople through your shared interests before discussing professional backgrounds. It helps build trust, which often leads to a mutually beneficial relationship.

The Payoff

Is investing time and energy in building a viable network worth it? Is there a pot of gold at the end of this rainbow? The answer is an emphatic YES! Leaders who are skilled at networking have access to people, resources, and information to help solve problems and create opportunities. It encourages personal growth, benefits organizations, and positively impacts the community. Although there are obviously more, here are **seven positive results** to be gleaned from establishing and growing a dynamic network:

1. **Access to personal development and coaching will help you grow and keep you engaged.** Most leaders I know say development and coaching are lacking in their organizations today. A dynamic network gives you access to new ideas, current trends, and ongoing opportunities to engage with a group of peers or mentors. This flow of information can help you and your organization stay ahead of the competition.

2. **Your influence will grow.** Time spent on growing and nurturing professional networks inside and outside your organization will greatly enhance your personal influence and effectiveness as a leader. People are more likely to buy in to what you are saying and doing if you have built a trusting relationship with them.

3. **Get ahead of the ongoing war for talent.** The generational landscape is rapidly changing, and the Great Resignation has turned the labor force upside down. Networking provides awareness of (and potential access to) talented professionals on whom you can call if you need to go outside your organization to hire. Stay connected within your industry, know the players, and develop trusted networking resources to help find the best talent.

4. **You can do immense good in the community.** Investing time in getting your connections to support your causes

(and in return support theirs) is a great way to exponentially leverage positive influence to serve the needs of others.

5. **You can help your extended network with their business and career needs if you are highly networked.** Connecting others to new jobs, positive business relationships, and the like is an excellent strategy that helps others and develops goodwill, which then may flow your way in the future.

6. **Your business will benefit from a network built on a foundation of authentic relationships.** If you are in sales or business development, view networking as a desire to do business with your friends rather than taking a transactional approach. I have seen firsthand that you will be exposed to more viable opportunities after you take the time to genuinely know someone and invest in the relationship.

7. **If you are in a job search, a strong network will help you.** In these volatile economic times, it is unfortunately likely that you will be in career transition one day. You owe it to yourself and your family to prepare for that possibility.

Helpful Tip: An important underlying theme of effective networking is *paying it forward*. Make your efforts about helping others and serving their needs, and you will find networking to be a worthwhile, fulfilling experience that will ultimately serve your needs as well. Remember: when it is all about you, people see through that, and networking becomes a miserable, laborious experience on many levels.

To conclude, I would suggest that leaders who neglect their networks are missing out on a critical component of their roles. By integrating networking as a fundamental aspect of your leadership and by proactively developing and nurturing networking-related skills, you create benefits for your team, your organization, and yourself. Randy Patterson, a senior HR executive and committed networker shared this insight with me:

> Making the personal commitment to truly building and cultivating my network has been one of the best decisions of my life. In addition to building knowledge to solve business problems or helping me to find great talent for my organization, networking has introduced me to many friends who I will keep for the rest of my life.

I practice what I preach. Until the pandemic hit, for more than twenty years I was typically at a restaurant called La Madeleine near the Perimeter Mall in Atlanta at 7:00 a.m. for coffee five days a week. I have shifted my habits during this post-pandemic phase of life, and I now schedule two to three coffee meetings a week near my home with clients, friends, and networking contacts. I am on Zoom most days and have additional and ample opportunities through this medium to connect with my network as well. I have spent many years building my network and am grateful for the highly synergistic relationships my colleagues and I have developed to help our respective businesses, the community and one another.

Your next great employee, business opportunity, Big Idea, opportunity to influence, community impact story, or career move may only be a coffee or Zoom meeting away. It's time to get started!

As you digest the best practices and ideas in this chapter, give yourself an honest grade on the state of your network and the quality of your business relationships. Are you meeting enough new professionals? Is this a priority? Give yourself a goal of connecting with three new professionals and reconnecting with or nurturing three existing relationships a month for three months. After three months, consider increasing the numbers. Find an accountability partner to challenge you and hold you accountable.

CHAPTER 16

The Right Way to Ask for What You Want in the Business World

*Asking for help isn't just about what you say and do;
it's also about what you don't say and do.*

HEIDI GRANT, SOCIAL PSYCHOLOGIST AND AUTHOR

How do we appropriately ask for what we want from others in the business world? Is there a right way and a wrong way? I am approached somewhat frequently by job seekers and business development professionals seeking to sell me something or hoping to gain access to new clients through my network. These requests for help are from both professionals in my network as well as from people I don't know. Some requests evoke an immediate favorable response from me. Some make me hesitate and carefully consider if I will help and still others make me cringe because of the way I am approached. Why the broad spectrum of reactions?

Before writing this chapter, I chatted with a few other professionals about their experiences on this topic and also analyzed the last several requests for assistance I have received.

What I learned from this exercise is that many people seeking help are often not self-aware and fail to recognize how they come across to others. They often have a genuine need for help, but the way the need is communicated may come across as one-sided, self-serving, and at times obnoxious.

Below are my recommendations to other professionals seeking help and how to do it in such a way that will likely get a favorable reply.

BEST Practices for Seeking Help

- **Be courteous.** I am amazed at the lack of common courtesy in some of the requests I receive. Saying "please" and "thank you" and "I am grateful" should be a given, but often it is not.
- **Offer help before asking for help.** A vital offshoot of courtesy is to make sure the person receiving the request knows that you desire to help them as well.
- **Provide context.** If you don't know the person, let them know how you found them and why you think they can help you.
- **Do your homework.** Know as much as possible about the person you are seeking help from before reaching out. Doing research and sharing some of what you learn in your communication makes the approach seem less random and will evoke a warmer response.
- **Spotlight what you may have in common.** How are you connected? Are there friends in common? Shared interests or organizations? Attend the same school?
- **Be clear and direct.** Don't make the person being asked for help do any legwork. Be clear about what you're asking for or

who you are looking to meet through this person. Remove the guesswork. If you are a job seeker (the most common requests I receive are from this group), ask if you can forward your resume and target company list. This is very helpful.

Below are examples of negative practices I have observed from other professionals seeking help.

WORST Practices for Seeking Help

- **Don't be respectful of time and calendars.** The person you are reaching out to may be extremely busy, and your need likely will not be their top priority. Acknowledge your respect for their valuable time as you make your request.
- **Act like you are old friends with people you barely know or don't know at all.** A common complaint from other professionals is help requests from people they haven't seen in years or have never met who act like their best friend. It comes across as false and is an immediate turnoff.
- **Make it all about you.** Don't make your request about only your issues and needs. Inquire about the other person and how they are doing. Make it clear you have a sincere interest in them.
- **Use a shotgun approach.** One of the most ineffective methods of asking for help is the blind copy approach where someone requests that we "keep them in mind if we see any interesting opportunities that fit their background." Another variation is to email someone directly with "I would love to meet anyone in your network who needs a good operations guy." This is impersonal, ineffective, and not likely to bring a positive result.

- **Send an unsolicited request to connect on LinkedIn with minimal information.** LinkedIn is a wonderful tool for building a network, but don't send random requests to connect without providing a reason. Always send a note explaining why you wish to connect. Positive examples: "We have several mutual friends," or "We worked together at ABC Company several years ago," or "I read an article in which you addressed connecting strategies. I have shared this with several friends and would like to connect with you if you don't mind."
- **Fail to follow up and show gratitude.** This request for help may not be the only time you reach out to this individual. Follow up with the results of their assistance and absolutely let them know you are grateful.

Here is an example of a request for assistance (from a job seeker) that is likely to receive a favorable response:

Bill,

Good morning. We have not met in person, but I recently learned that our children attend the same middle school, and Mike Baxter is a mutual friend. Mike spoke very highly of you and suggested that I reach out regarding my job search. I recognize how busy you are, but would you be open to me sending my resume and target list of companies? Do you have any time over the next two weeks to have a phone conversation or even a coffee or lunch meeting? I am very flexible regarding a call or meeting and will meet you anywhere that is convenient to your home or office.

I have an extensive network of senior executives and

would be very happy to help you with connections to this group if you would find it helpful. Please let me know if you do. At the risk of being premature, I would also like to invite you to join my LinkedIn network so you can see my profile and connections. I will forward this request on later today. You have my sincere thanks for considering this request. Is there anything I can do to prepare for our conversation to make it more productive?

With gratitude,

Maryanne Smith

This example is likely to get a favorable response from me and other professionals as it addresses most of the important issues. As you reflect on this chapter, put yourself in the shoes of the person on the other end of your request. How would you respond to requests straight from the "WORST Practices" list? If you are not certain about how you come across, reach out to the last few people you have solicited assistance from and ask the question: "How did you perceive my request and are there ways I could have improved it?"

We all need to ask for help from time to time. *How* we ask for this assistance is critical, and increasingly it seems that many of us are forgetting the fundamentals of effective business communication. Nobody is discounting the genuine need for the active assistance of others in a job search, the desire for new customers, the need for advice, or whatever is behind the need to make these requests, but taking the time to gauge our approach and the potential response on the other end can make all the difference in helping this effort be more successful. **Two key points**:

1. **We all have an opportunity to respectfully coach people who seek help on ways they can improve.** It can be immensely beneficial for them to receive this feedback.
2. **We can all likely make some improvements on how we seek help from others.** Let's be humble and open to change.

Reflect on the last several requests you have received for help in the business world. How did these professionals approach you? How did the requests make you feel? How did you respond? Consider how you have asked others for help in the last few months. Did you employ approaches from the BEST Practices list or the WORST Practices list? Where can you make adjustments to your approach to be more effective?

CHAPTER 17

Uncovering Normalized Defects

It's uncomfortable to challenge the status quo.
SETH GODIN

Most of us remember (or have read about) the tragic explosions of the space shuttles Challenger (1986) and Columbia (2003) and the deaths of all crew members in both accidents. As you may recall, NASA's investigation into both explosions uncovered problems that had been long known in the space shuttle program, ranging from faulty O-ring seals (Challenger) to foam insulation falling off during launches (Columbia). These problems, or defects, were widely known by front-line employees and expected to occur. NASA accepted these defects as part of the space shuttle launch process. Questions were raised, to be sure, but the questions lacked the kind of disciplined attention necessary to stop the problems from occurring. This has come to be known as the "normalization of defects."

My friend Steve Moore, author and president of Growing Leaders, introduced me to this concept through leadership work he has done in the past on this topic. Steve made the clear connection between the normalization of defects uncovered at NASA and the challenge of accepting defects in the business world. Curious, I wanted to go deeper.

Consider that a problem or defect may be observed so often that it fails to generate appropriate questions; thus, the desire to change it becomes diluted. Because it is *normal* to expect the problem, questions go unasked, and the problem is accepted as "the way we do things." If a business can list *normal* problems, it is guilty of *normalizing defects*. The result is a form of dysfunction and often significant limits are placed on the individual, team, and organization's ability to thrive and reach full potential.

Do we ever consider the defects that have become "normalized" in our organization? What bad habits have we accepted as a normal way of doing business that we know are wrong? What toxic behaviors have we tolerated and allowed to negatively influence our teams or overall company culture? Sometimes these defects can be a flawed process in a manufacturing plant or a software bug in an inventory tracking system, but more often than not they are human behaviors that we can control if we have the courage to confront and correct them.

In my experience, these are **six of the most common normalized defects** I have observed in business:

1. **Lack of candor** that results in an overly nice and political approach to conversations, which waters down or avoids the (sometimes) difficult truth that often needs to be shared.
2. **Lack of accountability** for results when leaders accept squishy timelines and vague commitments instead of

clear deadlines with specific and measurable deliverables. This is also revealed in the playing of favorites, with poor performance sometimes inexplicably overlooked or tolerated.

3. **Lack of time.** Unchecked busyness and a packed meeting calendar are the bane of existence for most of the leaders I know, and this negatively impacts their ability to think strategically, be creative, and invest in developing their people; it also contributes to burnout.

4. **Silos.** Silos exist everywhere in companies. Silos impede collaboration, negatively impact communication, and contribute significantly to organizational dysfunction. Often, a significant contributor to silos is the failure of leaders and their teams to forge effective and collaborative business relationships across their organization.

5. **Ignoring the necessity of critical feedback.** On an ongoing basis, effective leaders should seek out honest, specific, and critical feedback on their personal performance. They also have the responsibility to create a safe environment for team members to share this feedback. When done consistently well, this can inform a leader of his or her own defects and increase their overall effectiveness.

6. **Ignoring the bad behavior of top performers.** A common problem, known but not often acknowledged, is the tolerance of poor behavior or shortcuts to the process for team members who deliver strong revenue results.

What can we do to address the normalization of defects in

our own companies? First of all, *be patient*. It is easy to feel overwhelmed with the thought of rooting out and eliminating every defect. Pursue the low-hanging fruit and the easy-to-spot issues that you know have been ignored. If you are a leader with a genuine desire to make changes, consider these **five practical actions** to get started:

1. **Practice Honest Self-Reflection.** Look in the mirror. Reflect on your own behaviors and those of your team and greater organization. Where are the normalized defects? What defects can you address that are within your control?

2. **Ask the Team.** Bring the topic of defects up in one-on-one sessions, team meetings, and even town halls. Make it safe for colleagues to state what they think is broken or defective in how your organization is operating and thank them for their candid feedback. Never, ever, shoot the messenger!

3. **Prioritize.** In addition to being patient, it is more important to prioritize and address the urgent defects in bite-sized chunks. Make this priority list an ongoing agenda item for all conversations going forward until the defects are addressed.

4. **Look for Obvious Clues.** Dive deeper and investigate when you hear comments like the following:

   - "That's just the way we have always done things here."
   - "Keep that stuff to yourself. Our senior execs don't want to hear anything negative."

- "Mike has always been really hard on his people. That's just his style."
- "We can't ever get the information we need from Kathy's team."
- "The project team missed the deadline again, but they are really busy."
- "You better watch your step in Bill's meeting. He hates bad news."
- "I know what Janet did was wrong, but we can't afford to lose her revenue contribution."

5. **Be Courageous.** Identifying and uprooting defects—both our own and those of the organization—will not be easy. We will likely encounter significant resistance because nobody likes to hear that they made mistakes or that by turning a blind eye to defects, they are negatively affecting themselves, their team, and the organization. Let's have the courage to be self-reflective and engage in honest conversations about what defects we have allowed to become normalized and then root them out. Not doing so means we, our teams and our organizations will continue to fall short of our potential and possibly even court disaster. Encourage the dialogue to begin and be brave enough to get started.

After reading this chapter, what resonated most? Where are the normalized defects in your company or team? Enlist the help of your colleagues and hold each other accountable for progress. A proven approach to move forward looks like this:

- *Share this chapter (or the main ideas) with your team to help them get familiar with the idea of normalized defects.*
- *In a team meeting, spend twenty minutes identifying all the normalized defects that are directly connected to the work of you and your team. Give everyone permission to be candid and promote psychological safety to make people more comfortable speaking up.*
- *Break the team into groups (three to five people, if possible) and put them into virtual breakout rooms or conference rooms if you are meeting in person. Assign each team one normalized defect. Give each team twenty-five minutes to brainstorm a specific action plan to solve their defect and then invite them to present their plan to the rest of the team. Require their plans to be as specific as possible.*
- *After any necessary refining, put the plans into action.*
- *Continue the exercise above over the months ahead to work through the list of defects and address new ones as they are identified.*

PART THREE

Being Good
Humans

CHAPTER 18

Basic Humanity Gets a Boost on the Hiking Trail

Interdependence is and ought to be as much the ideal of man as self-sufficiency. Man is a social being.

Mahatma Gandhi

As is our custom most weekends, my older son, Alex, and I went hiking not long ago on a Saturday afternoon at a park with excellent trails near our home. I find this time in the woods to not only be excellent father/son time, but an opportunity to work on my health, disengage from the hectic world around me, and be more thoughtful and reflective. As we walked the hilly trails, my thoughts turned to the damaging impact the pandemic has had the last two years on relationships and the overall state of disconnectedness many of us feel. I have also observed with concern the accelerated deterioration of common courtesy, gratitude, and mutual respect during this time that was already in motion long before COVID-19 turned our lives upside down. I am not sure I have ever experienced a more divisive, angrier period in my adult life. This line of thinking, to be honest, put me in a bit of a gloomy mood during the hike until my son and I had three random encounters that changed my perspective for the better.

Three Encounters

Halfway through the trail, Alex and I ran into the father-in-law of a friend of mine accompanied by three of his young grandsons. They were going fishing in the pond at the center of the park, and I have rarely seen a more joyful group. I have known this gentleman for several years, and we struck up a casual conversation about family, business, and life in general. He told his grandsons who I was, and much to my surprise, each of the boys extended their hand in greeting, introduced themselves, told me their name and age and said, "It was nice to meet you, Mr. Hain." Knowing something of the values and character of this man's family, I should not have been surprised. Still, I was impressed and gratified to see the teaching influence of the boys' parents and grandparents at work in how they displayed sincere courtesy and respect at such a young age and how much they enjoyed each other's company. My mood began to improve as I continued with Alex on the trail and bid the happy family goodbye.

A little further along, Alex and I encountered a married couple who commented on the Samford University sweatshirt I was wearing. They asked me if I had attended Samford, and I shared that my younger son, Ryan, was a senior at the school. This led to a friendly conversation about their college-age kids, the challenges our children faced during the pandemic with hybrid classrooms, and our shared concern about their career and life prospects in today's world. As I often mentor college students about life and careers, I gave them my card and asked them to have their kids reach out to me if I could be of any assistance. They thanked me profusely, and the father shared with me that he was a senior executive at the company where my younger son happened to have an upcoming summer internship. When he learned about my son's upcoming job, he quickly offered to reach out to my son and ensure that he had a good internship experience. What started out as a friendly conversation between absolute strangers, inspired by a college logo on a sweatshirt, turned into the potential for helpful mutual assistance for our college-age kids. My mood brightened even more as Alex and I left the friendly couple.

As we continued our walk, with me deep in thought and reflecting on the lessons of these two encounters, I was startled by a loud "Good afternoon!" I looked up to see an elderly gentleman with a walking stick smiling warmly at me and Alex. He remarked in accented English that it was a beautiful day, and I shared his observation that, indeed, it was wonderful weather for a hike. He seemed eager to engage in conversation and shared that he had emigrated to the United States from Thailand a few years ago to be near his children and grandchildren. Sadly, his wife passed away about a year ago. We had little in common except, perhaps, a mutual desire to simply have a conversation and relate to each other as good human beings. I shared a little about my life in return before wishing him a good afternoon. The warmth of his smile and sincere kindness will stay with me for a while, and I am grateful to have met him.

Moments of Hope

I thoughtfully reflected on these random encounters along

the hiking trail as I drove home with Alex. It dawned on me that if we can slow down and experience life in real time, we can enjoy more of these teaching moments that will open our eyes and perhaps touch our hearts. Moments like these can also give us hope and fortify us for the unpredictable life journey in front of us. It is worthy to note that, as we consider the world we live in today, none of these encounters involved a discussion about politics or which side we were on regarding other sensitive issues. We simply reached out across the man-made barriers that often separate people and made connections. We attempted to be good human beings on a Saturday afternoon in the middle of the woods, and I would suggest we succeeded. It is not far-fetched to recognize that there is so much more that we have in common as cohabitants of this planet than what sets us apart.

I am hopeful that the painful days of lockdowns and mask mandates are permanently behind us. I encourage you to reconnect in meaningful ways to those you have become physically distant from over the last few years. I believe people are craving deeper connection and eagerly seeking it. Most importantly, I humbly challenge you to treat everyone you encounter at work and in the community with more kindness, courtesy, and respect. Reject anger, frustration, and divisiveness and instead embrace compassion, mercy, and forgiveness. Relationships, genuine connection, and a sense of true community require people to be curious, active listeners, to care about and desire what is truly best for one another. We are all members of the human race, and we have an obligation and duty to look for the good in others and treat one another well.

My faith in humanity received a little boost out on the hiking trail. If you can slow down and be present, savor your encounters with others and break down the unnecessary walls that divide us, this can be your experience as well. Be brave and go for a walk after you read this and see who crosses your path.

In the days ahead, be intentional about scheduling time with someone you have not talked to in the last year or so. Try to meet with them in person if possible and reconnect. Consider all of your encounters at work and elsewhere as opportunities to build productive relationships, regardless of backgrounds, race, gender, or different points of view. Engage, listen, look for the good . . . and see what happens.

CHAPTER 19

Regular Heroes

Some believe it is only great power that can hold evil in check, but that is not what I have found. It is the small everyday deeds of ordinary folk that keep the darkness at bay. Small acts of kindness and love. Why Bilbo Baggins? Perhaps because I am afraid, and he gives me courage.

(Gandalf) J.R.R. Tolkien, *The Hobbit*

A blog post I received a few months before the publication of this book contained a reference to the "ministry of obscurity." I found this to be quite profound if we apply that label to the millions of people around the world laboring every day to do good in their communities, being kind to others, raising their families, loving their neighbors, sharing their faith with others, caring for the sick, poor, and neglected, protecting us from harm, and leading virtuous lives—all in relative obscurity and seeking no recognition for their noble efforts. They are beacons of light in an increasingly angry and polarized world. Thinking about them gives me hope.

Through the countless conversations I have with others in my community and professional network, it is obvious that many of us feel let down and frustrated by politicians and public figures who espouse the right things but whose actions don't align with their words. Perhaps we are looking in the wrong places. Maybe for too long we have placed the wrong people on pedestals. It is entirely possible that we need look no further than our own families, workplaces, and communities for regular heroes to inspire us with their good examples.

They are all around us, but we may fail to notice them as it is easy to overlook the hardworking, virtuous, and generous among us. We may not always observe their good work because they go about doing the right things in often quiet ways, avoiding the spotlight whenever possible. They care more about doing good than getting the credit. When they are not working, they are likely spending quality time with their loved ones, serving others in the community, or investing in those they mentor. They provide a powerful witness in the simplest of actions.

What prompted me to write this chapter? In the weeks after I began pondering the idea of the ministry of obscurity, I encountered three people whom I had the good fortune to see—*maybe for the first time*—as regular heroes quietly serving in this ministry. I have known who they are for years, but I was struck recently by how they are such good role models for me and others who know them.

Tom, a successful senior executive devoted to his church and his family, selflessly gives his time to a local homeless shelter each month and organizes his church community to support it. He is a quiet and humble man who can always be counted on when someone needs help . . . and he coaches his daughter's soccer team for good measure.

Allison, a talented mid-level manager with a well-known

consulting company, quietly devotes as much time as possible to helping job seekers and mentoring other young professionals. She juggles all of this as a newlywed with the demands of a hectic job and has recruited her husband to help.

Finally, there is Sandy, the grandmother of a young man on the autism spectrum. Sandy started a nonprofit to help amazing young people like her grandson learn to communicate more effectively through improv and theater classes adapted to their style of learning. Her nonprofit has helped hundreds of people on the autism spectrum, and she is an inspiration to all who know her. There was a need that was not being addressed in the autism community and she took it upon herself to tackle it.

Regular heroes such as these three individuals and others like them are often humble, selfless, and focused on how they can serve others. They are not necessarily trying to change the world, but instead focus on helping one person at a time. Here are **five ways** we can recognize them:

1. They are **joyful** and **peaceful**, which naturally draws others to them.
2. They live **authentic** and **courageous** lives that do not change to suit their companions or in the face of life's challenges.
3. They have a **generous spirit**; when engaging with others, it is always about you and not about them.
4. The folks I know who fit this category see their service to others as a **duty** and **privilege** that they are happy to carry out.
5. Their good work transcends politics and cultural whims.

Doing the right thing for anyone in need is all that matters.

These regular heroes don't care who gets the credit. They pursue "eulogy virtue" versus "resume virtue," as described by author David Brooks in his book, *The Road to Character*.[4] Both types of virtues are important and worth pursuing and refining, but only eulogy virtues have any lasting value and legacy. For them, it's not about the glory or the fame. It's just a wonderful way to live.

I shared three examples of regular heroes laboring in the "ministry of obscurity" who grabbed my attention when I stopped seeking inspiration from those in the public arena and began looking at my own backyard and the people I encounter in my daily life. There are so many examples I could have also cited, such as the single mom working two jobs to support her young family, the foster parents who routinely take in and help troubled teens, and the teenager who organizes his friends to pick up trash on weekends to protect the environment and beautify his community. Who are the regular heroes in your world? What valuable lessons can you learn from them? We should seek them out, share our sincere gratitude, and hopefully follow their great example.

Thank you to all who make the world a better place in your own quiet ways.

Consider the "regular heroes" in your life. What can you learn from them? How can you emulate their example? Keep a log of how many good acts you intentionally

---

4 David Brooks, *The Road to Character* (New York: Random House, 2016).

perform for two weeks where you receive no recognition other than directly from the recipients of your deeds. Reflect on how you feel after doing this and the positive impact you may have made on others.

CHAPTER 20

We Should All Be More Like Dave

*About once a month I run across a person who radiates an inner light.
These people can be in any walk of life. They seem deeply good. They
listen well. They make you feel funny and valued. You often catch them
looking after other people and as they do so their laugh is musical and
their manner is infused with gratitude. They are not thinking about
what wonderful work they are doing. They are not thinking about
themselves at all. When I meet such a person it brightens my whole day.
But I confess I often have a sadder thought: It occurs to me that I've
achieved a decent level of career success, but I have not achieved that. I
have not achieved that generosity of spirit, or that depth of character.*

David Brooks, *The Road to Character*

I was reminiscing with my younger son not long ago about the
2021 NBA playoff game we attended in our home city. The
arena was packed that night, and the atmosphere was electric
as 15,000-plus fans eagerly awaited the beginning of the game.
As I waited for the tip off, I noticed an elderly gentleman and a
teenage boy enter the row in front of us as they looked for their
seats. The older man introduced himself as Dave to people as
he walked by and proudly let everyone know that the young
man with him was his youngest grandson, Michael.

As our team fell behind in the game, my attention was drawn to Dave and the conversations he was having with those around him. The group that surrounded Dave was generationally and racially diverse, resembling an American melting pot of sorts. He engaged everyone in his vicinity with a warm smile, polite banter, courteous questions, and comments on the game. He also shared a few funny stories and talked about his family and his lifetime love affair with basketball. Nobody seemed to mind. In fact, the crowd seemed to genuinely enjoy being around this delightful and joy-filled man. When the game ended, he sincerely thanked everyone for making the game more enjoyable for him and his grandson.

What struck me as interesting about this encounter with Dave was the contrast it demonstrates in our country today with the division and hatred we constantly hear about through the media and groups with questionable agendas. I have no doubt this exists in pockets all over, but through the example of Dave and countless other experiences I have had, I know there is also a great deal of love, joy, kindness, and mutual respect in the world. *Division and hatred are* not *our predetermined destiny*. We have a clear choice to make about how we engage with one another, and there is no reason we can't choose civility, kindness, respect, and even love in our daily encounters.

I absolutely see the complexity of the problem, but I also believe in the simplicity of the solution. Today (and every day), you and I will have opportunities to engage with someone who doesn't look like us, sound like us, share our beliefs, or look at the world as we do. We must remember that we are all human beings and fellow travelers on this earth. As writer

G.K. Chesterton once said, "We are all in the same boat in a stormy sea, and we owe each other a terrible loyalty."

You and I will not solve the problems of the world by ourselves, but that doesn't mean we can't act. We can emulate Dave and the other good examples we likely have observed in our daily lives. We can choose to engage everyone with a smile, assume good intent, look for common ground, and hopefully reflect whatever joy we may be feeling toward others. Let's reject the noise and choose to build a world where this is the norm, not the exception. St. Teresa of Calcutta (Mother Teresa) is often quoted as saying, "I alone cannot change the world, but I can cast a stone across the waters to create many ripples." At an NBA playoff game where I happened to be present, a man named Dave created positive ripples that left a strong impression on me and the people around him. Maybe we should all be more like Dave.

As you reflect on this brief chapter, consider what strikes you as interesting about Dave and the audience around him. I would suggest that Dave clearly exuded joy, warmth, and kindness . . . and the people around Dave were clearly drawn to him and his personality. His authentic example is a good one for all of us to follow. Can we try to intentionally emulate this behavior in the days ahead?

CHAPTER 21

Thoughtfully Considering Generosity

It is every man's obligation to put back into the world at least the equivalent of what he takes out of it.

Albert Einstein

Generosity is one of my favorite words and a trait I greatly admire in others. I would like to share some thoughts with you on generosity that will encourage you to pause and reflect, but also hopefully influence how you live the rest of this year and beyond. Would you agree that generosity inspires gratitude, and gratitude inspires generosity? Let me share a brief story that illustrates this point.

An admirer of the great German composer Johannes Brahms left him a large sum of money in his will. Upon learning of the generous gift, the composer was deeply moved. "It touches me most deeply and intimately," he wrote to a friend. "All exterior honors are nothing in comparison." Then, in the next sentence, he shared that since he did not need the money, he was "enjoying it in the most agreeable manner, by taking pleasure in its distribution."

The generosity that was shown to Brahms was immediately passed along by the composer to those in need. The virtue of generosity that affected Brahms inspired replication of itself in the generosity that Brahms himself demonstrated to others. We would also hope that it stirred the same virtue among the beneficiaries of his gifts. When we consider that there is a *ripple effect* resulting from our generosity, we may be compelled to be more thoughtful and focused on giving to those we engage with each day. If we reflect more deeply on this, it is clear that generosity is the virtue that can go on mirroring itself forever.

The greatest gift we can give to another is the gift of ourselves. Giving of ourselves in this way epitomizes the virtue of generosity. The impulse toward generosity is implanted in the depth of man's being from our very creation. Consequently, to live a truly authentic life means to give generously to others. For those of us who are Christians, we know God's gift of Himself through Christ represents the ultimate form of generosity and serves as a model for all human generosity. We are reminded of this tremendous gift to the world every year in the celebration of Christmas.

Considered as a virtue, does generosity have limits? Since virtue is rooted in love, this question is similar to us asking, "Does love have limits?" If we indulge the analytical side of our brains, being generous seems to be costly and perhaps uncomfortable at times. If we live with a generous heart, acting from a place of greed seems almost incomprehensible. It is greed that makes us poorer, not generosity. True generosity, when practiced consistently and well, enriches our lives beyond measure. I believe there is an abundance of generosity within each of us, waiting to come out. Not to release it is to cost us a little of who we are. Nothing, therefore, is more costly than greed. Nothing is more rewarding than generosity.

If we consider famous literary characters such as Ebenezer Scrooge and The Grinch, we will realize they were driven by greed in such a way that the greedier they become, the less human they appear. The ultimate conversions of Scrooge and The Grinch are, in effect, returns to humanity that are joyfully appreciated by the reader. People living lives firmly rooted in generosity are not only more likable than those who are greedy, but they also appear to be more human and certainly more authentic. Do you agree?

It is more blessed to give than to receive, but it is far more blessed to give than to take. For a moment, let's thoughtfully consider how the gift of our time, our willingness to listen, our patience, our mercy, our talents, our kindness, our love, and our financial resources can be applied to more intentionally living the virtue of generosity toward others. In the end, we cannot take with us what we have, though many of us seem to live as though we could. But we can joyfully share what we have been given, accumulated, or earned with the people we encounter each day. Finally, remember that generosity is a virtue for everyone—not only for the prosperous and blessed. Generosity can take many forms, and everyone has an opportunity to enjoy the fruits of this virtue, regardless of their struggles or situation in life.

Who will benefit from your generosity today?

As you ponder the points in this chapter, I encourage you to be more intentional about the practice of generosity in the days ahead. Think about how to improve this practice at work, with family, with friends, and in your community. A great way to grow in generosity is to quietly think at the beginning of every encounter, How can I best serve and help this person? and see the goodness that follows.

CHAPTER 22

The Attractiveness of Joy

There are two ways of spreading light: to be the candle or the mirror that reflects it.

EDITH WHARTON, PULITZER PRIZE-WINNING AUTHOR

I recently spoke with a senior leader in my business network on the topic of inspiring and encouraging employees after what has been a very challenging few years. As we shared observations, we were both struck by how gloomy, cynical, and anxious many leaders (and their team members) in our extended networks seem to be about life, work, and what lies ahead. This is certainly understandable in light of what we have experienced with the pandemic years, politics, social unrest, the economy, overwhelming negativity from news channels and social media, and a host of other challenges that are slowly wearing us down and making many of us feel more jaded.

If you will indulge me, I would like to offer a nonscientific antidote for business leaders who are feeling jaded. I know it is effective because I have seen it in action over most of my adult life. I strongly believe the best way to counter feeling jaded is to work at sincerely embracing a more *joyful mindset*. I hope we can agree that jaded leaders likely struggle to inspire and encourage others, but joyful leaders excel at it. For some leaders who embrace this joyful mindset, the change will be like flipping a switch. For others, it may require significant effort. Regardless, I promise the journey is worth it!

How exactly do we become more joyful leaders? I could ask this question of ten different people and get ten different answers. Perhaps it would help if I describe how I observe these leaders showing up to me and others. The most effective leaders I know act differently and embrace a joy-filled approach to work and life in general. There are consistent behaviors that form the foundation of a joyful mindset in these leaders—here are some examples:

- The joyful leaders I know are **grateful** for what they have and are not focused on what they may be missing.
- They are **humble** and strive to give others the credit for their successes.
- They are **authentic** and consistently true to who they are at all times, regardless of the audience.
- They handle adversity with **calmness**, **humor**, and a focus on **learning** from difficult moments.
- They are **generous** with their time and invest cheerfully and selflessly in their relationships with work colleagues, friends, and family.
- They **give back** to their community and serve and support great causes.
- They are **realistic** about challenges; they don't ignore them but rather choose to be **optimistic** and **hopeful** about solving them.

- They **practice self-care** and are intentional about taking care of their physical, emotional, spiritual, and mental needs. They understand that we cannot share with others from an empty cup.
- The most joyful leaders I know have strong **faith** and recognize that their joy ultimately comes from God.

One other common behavior of the joyful leaders I know is how they consistently inspire and make others feel better, especially their work colleagues. I am reminded of this powerful quote attributed to St. Teresa of Calcutta (Mother Teresa):

Let anyone who comes to you go away feeling better and happier. Everyone should see goodness in your face, in your eyes, in your smile. Joy shows from the eyes. It appears when we speak and walk. It cannot be kept closed inside us. It reacts outside. Joy is very infectious.

As we ponder this idea of being jaded or joyful, think about the role we can play in preparing for a more positive, hopeful, and joyful future. We can fight the widespread gloom that surrounds us by spreading goodwill and joy in our daily interactions with others. We can greet others with kindness and a smile and serve their needs as best we can. We can speak with work colleagues, friends, and family with the desire to bring joy and cheerfulness to the conversation rather than complaints or negativity. We can go out of our way to help and serve those who may be struggling in our companies, families, and communities. Wouldn't you agree that when we offer encouragement and joy to others, we are quietly fueling growth in these critical areas for ourselves as well?

Maybe all of these noble efforts can help us provide the inspiration and encouragement our work colleagues (and others) need from us right now. Maybe we will embrace this thinking because we recognize that we are beyond ready to abandon our jaded mindset and need this simple reminder. Whatever the reason, let's all do our part to create a ripple effect of joy in our spheres of influence. If we lead with joy, others will follow. Only good things will result when we do.

Reflect for a few minutes on your current mindset. Are you feeling jaded or joyful? Depending on your state of joy, commit to modeling and improving your practice of the key behaviors of joyful leaders mentioned in the chapter. Discuss your efforts with a friend or two and encourage one another's efforts to grow in this area.

CHAPTER 23

The (Often) Neglected Practice of Praise

Nothing else can quite substitute for a few well-chosen, well-timed, sincere words of praise. They're absolutely free and worth a fortune.

Sam Walton, founder of Wal-Mart

I was reminiscing the day after Father's Day this year about the many gifts and life lessons my father has shared with me over the years. He is quiet and humble in the way he carries himself, preferring to let his actions and good example do his talking for him. I observed one of his timeless lessons about a week ago, when he got on the phone with my oldest son, Alex, and praised him for his recent six-year employment anniversary at a well-known global retailer. The praise for my eldest son's big accomplishment was specific and encouraging, and my father ended the call with "I am very proud of you." Alex has high-functioning autism, but he responded to this warm and well-deserved praise as we all likely would with a big grin and a warm thank-you to his papa.

This call between a grandfather and grandson may not seem

remarkable, but I wonder how often we miss opportunities to praise the achievements, good work, or other positive behaviors we see from the people we encounter each day. Think beyond just our immediate families and consider our work colleagues, teachers at our children's schools, employees at the local grocery store, servers at our favorite restaurants, or the local police officers who keep our neighborhoods safe as relevant examples worthy of more praise. There is certainly plenty of condemnation, criticism, and negativity to be found, but it seems that sincere and positive praise may sometimes be lacking in today's world.

This is what good human beings should be doing...*and maybe we can all do better.*

Inspired by my father's example, I set out to be much more intentional with my praise in the days that followed. Here are some of the good people I encountered and the praise I tried to share as I sought to emulate my father's efforts:

- A client of mine had a breakthrough with a difficult team member as she followed my advice to get more personal and vulnerable instead of only focusing on work. She reached out via email right after the conversation to let me know of the employee's positive reaction, and we hopped on a quick call to debrief about the encounter. I listened a lot, sincerely praised her for the breakthrough, and encouraged her try again as soon as possible with her peers and other members of the team. She was rightly proud of herself, and I simply recognized this big step forward in her growth as a senior leader.
- The Publix near our home does a wonderful job of

employing adults with special needs. As the father of a son with autism, I am always grateful to see this when I enter the store and have the opportunity to engage with these amazing people. I sought out the store manager last week, shared my family's gratitude for his refreshing openness to providing these often-neglected members of society with gainful employment and praised him for his efforts. He seemed both grateful and surprised, sharing that he rarely received acknowledgment for what he described as "just trying to provide jobs for good people," and he reiterated his strong commitment to continuing his store's efforts in this area.

- My younger son and I had just traveled to Chicago for Father's Day weekend to see the Atlanta Braves play the Chicago Cubs at Wrigley Field. We had an amazing time. We also had a great experience with our hotel, especially with Charles, the elderly gentleman who greeted guests as they arrived and did whatever he could to make people feel welcome. He possessed an incredibly warm smile and inviting personality that reminded me of my own father. I shared with the hotel manager praise for Charles' work, attitude, and thoughtfulness toward his guests. I also thanked Charles personally, specifically letting him know why. He responded with a huge grin as he said, "It is truly my pleasure, and I hope you will be back. You just made my day. Happy Father's Day!" We will be back, and it will largely be because of this kind gentleman.

I share these little snippets, inspired by my father's good example, to illustrate how simple and easy it is to slow down and recognize others with well-deserved praise when we are more intentional. It cost me nothing, but it made a positive difference to the people who heard it. I have a lot of work to do in this area, but I am encouraged by the results and will keep trying. I would also suggest **four best practices** to embrace when ramping up your own praise efforts:

1. **Be measured and appropriate.** Not everything (or everyone) is amazing. Be discerning and make it sincere and sticky by looking for those behaviors, positive attitudes, and even small examples of good work that grab your attention and deserve a kind word of praise. "He who praises everybody, praises nobody" (Samuel Johnson).

2. **Be specific.** You are in a restaurant, for example, and wish to praise your server. Compare "You are doing an awesome job!" to "The food was fantastic today, and you did a great job serving our large party. We love your warmth and hospitality! Would you mind inviting the manager over so I can share our great experience with her?" Letting people in any of your daily encounters know exactly what was worthy of praise is likely to encourage them to continue that behavior.

3. **Be intentional.** Look for opportunities, as I tried my best to do last week, for ways to be more intentional in sharing praise with people you encounter. Put down the smartphone, take a deep breath, and look around more often. Live in the moment and think more deeply about who has been placed in your path, how they are showing up to you, and what they are doing. Thoughtfully consider how you could more frequently make someone's

day and sprinkle a little goodness in the world with the practice of more appropriate praise.

4. **Make it quiet or escalated.** Sometimes quiet one-on-one praise for the deserving person is all that is needed and is more than appropriate. But there are times when we want to escalate the praise to let someone's boss or others know of the great work we witnessed and make sure it gets appropriately noticed and rewarded.

It is easy to become trapped in our mental prisons, focused on our own worlds and not paying adequate attention to the people around us. I hope you will see that increasing your own praise efforts will have a positive ripple effect in those who receive it from you. It will serve as a helpful counter to the negativity and harshness that can be part of everyday life. Your thoughtful praise may create a spark in someone that could inspire them to do truly great things and maybe pass along sincere praise to others. My dad has been doing this well his whole life, and I know firsthand the difference he has made in the lives of others.

Our reward will most likely be a smile from the recipient and their obvious pleasure that someone noticed and took the time to acknowledge something worthy of praise. We can all likely do more in this area—let's give it a shot and make someone smile today.

As you ponder the message of this chapter, commit to sharing deserving praise with someone at work, home, and in your community at least once a day for two weeks. At the end of this period, reflect on how the effort has impacted you and the difference it made in the lives of those you praised. Integrate this practice into your daily routine.

CHAPTER 24

A Small Act of Chivalry

On that best portion of a good man's life,
His little, nameless, unremembered acts
Of kindness and of love.

WILLIAM WORDSWORTH, POET

As I look at today's world, something is very, very wrong. The level of anger and divisiveness is out of control. You rarely see people with opposing views reason together and have civil discussions to resolve their differences. Diversity of thought is often not welcomed. We don't hold people accountable for their bad behavior, and situations escalate to angry words and senseless violence in the blink of an eye. The rule of law is routinely being ignored, and traditional values and our core institutions are constantly being attacked. Kindness, courtesy, respect, and simple decency are becoming more and more scarce.

But, despite all of these challenges, there is also much that is good in the world. I was recently reminded of this truth when a friend shared this famous J.R.R. Tolkien quote from *The Return of the King*, which I first read many years ago:

There, peeping among the cloud-wrack above a dark tor high up in the mountains, Sam saw a white star twinkle for a while. The beauty of it smote his heart, as he looked up out of the forsaken land, and hope returned to him. For like a shaft, clear and cold, the thought pierced him that in the end the Shadow was only a small and passing thing: there was light and high beauty forever beyond its reach.[5]

This illustrates to me that the current state of society is not permanent. We can change things for the better, and in fact, men and women of goodwill are doing their part every day to make a positive difference. I believe these small acts of love, goodness, kindness, bravery, and virtue are ultimately what will help our nation and the world get back on track.

A Small but Inspiring Example of Chivalry

Not long ago, I was sitting at Mass with my family when I quietly observed an inspiring scene that lasted all of five minutes. Two rows in front of us was a young teenage girl sitting next to her older brother and the rest of her family. The girl sneezed a few times and clearly needed to blow her nose. In the row in front of me and sitting directly behind her was a man I know pretty well who was there with his family. He handed the young lady a clean cloth handkerchief he must have kept in his pocket for just such an emergency. She was clearly not sure if she should take it and looked to her older brother for guidance. He swiftly looked at the older man and then nodded to his sister that it was OK. She used the

5 J.R.R Tolkien, *The Return of the King* (New York: Random House, 1955), 211.

handkerchief, and then the embarrassment of what to do with the now dirty cloth hit her, and she looked lost and nervous. The brother took it from her, folded it carefully with the dirty part on the inside, and handed it back to the older gentleman while expressing his thanks. She turned around as well and, with a warm smile, mouthed a silent thank you.

Why is this short incident worthy of mention?

The older gentleman demonstrated courtesy and thoughtfulness to a young lady who will likely never forget his kind act. He acted as a gentleman should, and perhaps the young lady had not seen many examples of this behavior from the boys in her school. The older brother also witnessed from the older man how a true gentleman should behave and probably gleaned as much as his sister from what he observed. The following Sunday, I ran into the girl's father outside of our church and asked him if his daughter or son had relayed the incident. They had not, and I described the exchange for him. He drew the same conclusions as me about lessons learned and was grateful I told him. He also committed to thank the gentleman with the handkerchief, whom he knew as well.

It is sometimes the little acts of kindness that make a lasting impression. Letting young people witness kindness and generosity in the form of gentlemanly behavior could have a ripple effect both on how that young lady raises expectations for how she wishes to be treated by men in the future and how her older brother engages with the women in his life. Also, it is likely that the gentleman with the handkerchief simply derived pleasure at his small opportunity to be of service to a young lady in need. It inspired me to witness that chivalry is clearly not dead and there are some, like the man in the pew, who are keeping it alive.

After you read this chapter, consider how you can do one thing to make a positive difference in the world today. Don't allow yourself to feel overwhelmed by all that is going wrong. Just focus on the little things you can do and remember the sage words of Mother Teresa (St. Teresa of Calcutta): "We ourselves feel that what we are doing is just a drop in the ocean. But the ocean would be less because of that missing drop."

CHAPTER 25

Acts of Kindness, the Goodness of People, and Lessons Learned

I think probably kindness is my number one attribute in a human being. I'll put it before any of the things like courage, or bravery, or generosity, or anything else. . . . Kindness—that simple word. To be kind—it covers everything, to my mind. If you're kind, that's it.

Roald Dahl

As I have shared in other chapters, I am blessed to be the father of two wonderful sons. My oldest son is named Alex, and he has high functioning autism. Our family has countless stories and experiences describing how Alex has touched our lives and made us better people, but that is not the subject of this chapter. The words you are about to read are meant to pay homage to the incredible kindness of people who came into my son's life the year he graduated from high school, the gifts he received from these amazing individuals, and the lessons my family and I have drawn from these experiences ever since.

A Difficult Decision

In 2016, when our son was eighteen and in his senior year of high school, my wife and I made the difficult decision to delay college for Alex. He is very intelligent, but we felt his social and communications challenges would make the college experience overwhelming for him until he matured and developed the skills for coping with the demands associated with furthering his education. While we still hope for some form of college education is in his future, at the time we felt that life skills training and some sort of paid employment would be the appropriate next steps in his development.

As my wife researched life skills programs, I began talking to companies in the Atlanta area about employment opportunities for young adults on the autism spectrum. The conversations were frustrating to say the least, as few companies at that time were willing to take what they saw as a risk in employing adults with autism. I knew if they would only give Alex an opportunity, they would see his many positive qualities and how he could be a model employee with the right level of support.

"Will You Give This Young Man an Interview?"

My fruitless search took me up until the month before Alex's high school graduation, and I had very little to show for my efforts. In a somewhat desperate move, I sent an email with Alex's resume and a list of his skills to about fifty friends who are senior level leaders or business owners in the northern Atlanta suburbs where we live, asking them to keep their eyes open for job opportunities suitable for Alex. Every single person replied with kind wishes, many offered prayers, and all of them made a promise to keep their eyes open for him, but no real job opportunities materialized.

My wife and I were feeling a little desperate and frustrated as the days until graduation rapidly flew by and we still did not have the job portion of the post-high school plan in place for our son. On the Wednesday before Alex's graduation, I received a call from the HR manager at a nearby store, part of a well-established international retail company. She had received Alex's resume from someone at their corporate office with a simple request: "Will you give this young man an interview?" The HR manager asked if Alex could come to the store that Friday afternoon for an interview with the store manager. I quickly said yes . . . and asked if I could attend the interview to support Alex. As I hung up the phone, I smiled to myself as I remembered that one of the recipients of my email blast a few weeks before was a friend from our parish who is a senior leader in this company. *The first act of kindness from a friend had opened the door to a possible job for our son.*

"When Can You Start?"

At 3:00 p.m. on the Friday before Alex's high school graduation, we were sitting in the store manager's office for my son's first ever job interview. Fifteen minutes later, the store manager smiled at Alex and offered him a job as a store associate at ten dollars an hour and asked him when he could start. My son gave me a worried look, unsure of what to say, and I quickly accepted on his behalf. This store manager took a chance and decided to hire Alex, even though his company had no formal program for employing adults on the autism spectrum. *The second act of kindness, from the store manager we had never met before, gave my son the gift of employment.*

"I Know This Probably Isn't How You Typically Do Things . . ."

As we walked down the hall to the office of the HR Manager to have Alex fill out the required paperwork, I asked her for a favor. "I know this probably isn't how you typically do things, but would you consider typing a few sentences stating that you are offering Alex a job on your company letterhead? While we have been in your store this afternoon, our family has flown in from all over the country for Alex's graduation, and they are waiting for us at our house. It would be wonderful if he could walk in with his 'offer letter' to show our family." The HR manager brushed aside her tears and happily agreed to my request. Alex walked into our house thirty minutes later with his job offer letter in hand to show his relatives. He had a proud smile on his face as he basked in the glow of excited family members hugging him for this major milestone. *This third act of kindness from the HR manager helped my son make the connection that he had accomplished something very significant by landing his first job.*

"I Definitely Understand, as I Have Two Nephews . . ."

About ten days later, our new high school graduate was scheduled for his first in-store training session. Being the "helicopter parent" of a child with special needs, I prepared a one-page summary of coaching tips for Alex's new co-workers and supervisors to help him be successful in his new job . . . and of course I made ten copies to share! Upon our arrival, an older gentleman named Joe approached me, saying he had been assigned to Alex as his in-store coach. I quickly pulled Joe aside and reviewed my coaching tips. He listened respectfully to everything I had to share, and then sheepishly said, "Mr. Hain, I really appreciate this great information about your son. I have two nephews with autism, and those boys mean the world to me. I promise to take good care of Alex and help him do well here." I was somewhat shocked as I absorbed these words, and I knew instinctively that my son would be in great hands. I left the store filled with gratitude for Joe and the store's thoughtfulness in pairing this good man with my son. *This fourth act of kindness showed the thoughtfulness of the store's management team and HR in selecting Joe as Alex's coach and ensured the likelihood of Alex's success with an understanding man like Joe to guide him.*

A Legacy of Leadership

Alex got off to a great start in his new job, in large part to Joe and the employees of the store who quickly adopted him and made him feel welcome and supported. Joe even shared with me one day when I picked Alex up after work that he was one of their best employees, saying that he "was always on time, did everything asked of him, never 'gossiped at the water cooler,' and asked for more work upon the completion of his tasks." Who would not value this kind of employee? Alex even won a customer service award in his fourth month on the job when a customer sent a note to the manager praising him for his assistance in loading a purchase into her car.

A few months after Alex started his job, I was at an awards luncheon where the former chairman and CEO of the company where my son works was given a lifetime achievement award for his legacy of excellent leadership and his contributions to the Atlanta community. As I listened to this well-respected leader talk about the importance of leadership and how the company treated its team members, I could clearly see the example this former CEO set being followed by the management team in my son's store. I had a profound desire to thank this man for the legacy of his leadership, but quickly dismissed the idea as there were seven hundred people between us.

As I began making my way out of the luncheon, still thinking about a way to thank this leader, I ran into him as I rounded a corner outside the ballroom where the event was held. Feeling emboldened at this unexpected opportunity, I walked up, shook his hand, and asked if he would like to hear a brief story. He gave me a curious look and said OK, likely thinking I was a disgruntled customer (he still serves on the company's board of directors). I told him about how Alex was hired and how well he had been supported, and I sincerely thanked him for the legacy of his leadership in impacting the store manager's decision to hire Alex. I also shared how this job helped my son gain much-needed confidence and self-esteem. He teared up and thanked me for sharing Alex's story, and then he asked for the store manager's name as well as Alex's full name. Perhaps it was a coincidence, but we noticed the next week that Alex started receiving more hours at work. *The fifth act of kindness is reflected in the leadership philosophy of this CEO and how his example and passion for treating people well impacted the hiring decision of the store manager who took a chance on Alex.*

Lessons Learned

As I write this, Alex is in his seventh year of employment at the store and thriving. Upon reflection, there are **five lessons** I have learned from Alex's job experience that have had a profound effect on me and my family:

1. **Don't be afraid to ask for help.** If I had not sent the email asking my network to keep Alex in mind, this job would not have been possible.

2. **Trust in the essential goodness of people.** Several absolute strangers came out of nowhere that year to offer friendship, prayers, support, and patience in opening doors for Alex and helping him thrive in his first job.

3. **Practice random acts of kindness.** Doing (unexpected) charitable acts for those we may encounter may make a significant and unforeseen difference in their lives . . . like the kind acts performed for my son.

4. **It is important to invite people into your life and share your struggles, not just your triumphs.** Most of us hear about all of the great news from our circle of friends, but how often do we hear about difficulties and challenges? Sharing "real life" issues like Alex's job search might open the door to solutions we are not expecting.

5. **Go with your instincts.** My wife and I knew Alex was not ready for a college experience at that time of his life, and we bucked conventional wisdom and the expectations of everyone we know in choosing life skills training and job experience as the next step for him after high school. His obvious happiness, growing mastery of essential life lessons, and increasing self-confidence over the last several years have been very validating for us.

A Final Act of Kindness

I hope all of us will reflect on this series of events woven together by the kindness of others in their efforts to help my son and consider how we might, in turn, make a difference in the lives of those we encounter each day. I know Alex's experiences that year have had a profound impact on me and my family that will never be forgotten. There is one final act of kindness that deserves to be shared. It is perhaps the best of them all and is the perfect end to this heartwarming story. The Christmas after he landed the job, Alex bought Christmas gifts for his family with his own money—the money he earned from his new job. He took a special pride in being able to do this on his own for the people he loves. This final act of kindness was that the young man who benefited so much from the kind acts of others reflected their kindness back to his loved ones during that special time of year. Goodness, generosity, and kindness are not the exclusive gifts of those who are "normal" and strong, but also of those in our society we often marginalize and overlook because they are not just like us.

How did this chapter speak to you? Consider the small acts of kindness and the goodness of people in your daily life that perhaps you have previously overlooked or innocently ignored. How will it impact your own willingness to share kindness and goodness with others in the future?

CHAPTER 26

Fostering Greater Civility

Let me never fall into the vulgar mistake of dreaming that I am persecuted whenever I am contradicted.

RALPH WALDO EMERSON

I was surprised by a call I received a few days before I finished the manuscript for *Upon Reflection* from someone I have known for a few years. We have a few friends in common, do similar work, and bump into each other on occasion, but we would consider each other professional acquaintances and not friends. When we finished pleasantries, I asked him what I could do for him, and he responded, "You are one of the few people I think I can trust to give me an honest opinion on a controversial topic, and I would like to ask you a few questions if you are open to it." Intrigued, I told him I would be glad to help and intently listened to what he had to say.

He shared that based on what he knew about me from my writings and our mutual friends, he assumed I would have firm opinions about a very contentious topic that has caused anger and division in our country for many years. He said he

159

respected me and was very eager to hear my perspective. He admitted that he probably had the opposite view on the topic, but he wanted to understand where I was coming from and increase his level of understanding. I confirmed his assumption about my opinion and calmly shared my perspective. I carefully walked through my reasoning with him, gave him context, and walked through a few clear examples to emphasize my point. He asked a few questions along the way and seemed to be cautiously avoiding sounding defensive or frustrated. When I was finished, I asked him to explain his reasoning to help me understand his point of view as well.

The same conversation played out in reverse as he calmly walked me through his perspective, giving examples and sharing context. He genuinely seemed to appreciate my questions and before we knew it, our conversation had gone on for nearly an hour. I was admittedly surprised that we calmly listened to each other and exhibited mutual respect. Although there was probably some tension below the surface because of the nature of the topic, we were careful to keep our emotions in check and restrained any animosity that we both may have felt.

There was an awkward silence when he finished until I said aloud what we were both likely thinking: "What just happened?"

He shared that he was sick of the anger and divisiveness that has caused so much polarization in our country and decided to do something that was decidedly countercultural, hence his call to me. I agreed wholeheartedly and thanked him for the courage, calmness, and civility he showed in reaching out. I know I will not change my opinion on this particular topic, and I suspect he won't change his either, but we will agree to disagree, knowing we both heard each other out and improved our mutual understanding. We kept on chatting for another thirty minutes and were surprised to learn that we also had much in common. We agreed to continue the conversation over coffee in the coming weeks and I sincerely look forward to the discussion with someone who may become a new friend.

Why does this matter? I think we have all observed, hopefully with great concern, that difficult conversations like the one I just described rarely occur anymore. You see people's opinions dismissed or belittled because of their political or religious affiliation, the color of their skin, their gender, and other various reasons. There is a tendency to go from zero to angry when difficult and contentious topics are raised, with both sides pointing fingers and voices being raised . . . or senseless violence being the unfortunate result. There was a time when we debated ideas, shared different opinions, and found ways to compromise and collaborate for the greater good in our country. Are those days long gone? Will they ever return?

We may disagree with one another on a number of things, but we must respect one another's perspective and one another's right to share that perspective in a calm and reasonable way. Any person or group who tries to shut down discussion and the debate of ideas and thoughts makes themselves resemble tyrants and dictators who can't defend the hollowness and errors of their thinking. I think reasonable people have had enough.

A Recipe for Civility

The call I referred to at the beginning of the chapter holds many keys to improving civility. Here are **seven keys** to consider as you engage in future potentially difficult conversations:

1. **Start with mutual respect and courtesy.** The gentleman who reached out to me set the tone with respect and courtesy at the very beginning of our conversation, and it made a huge difference in our ability to have a calm and reasonable discussion. We also both chose to be personable and friendly, not disagreeable.

2. **Actively listen.** One of the greatest catalysts for productive conversations is to actively listen and show understanding. Don't impatiently listen until it is your turn to speak. Listen to understand the other person's point of view. "The greatest compliment that was ever paid me was when someone asked me what I thought and attended to my answer" (Henry David Thoreau).

3. **Free speech is a fundamental right for all, even if you don't like what someone says**. In a quote often erroneously attributed to Voltaire, Evelyn Beatrice Hall wrote: "I disapprove of what you say, but I will defend to the death your right to say it." You may not like what the other person is saying, but they absolutely have a right to say it, as do we all.

4. **We might learn something new.** Try being more curious and ask thoughtful questions. If we approach conversations with a desire to learn, we might gain new perspectives and deeper understanding. We might even change our minds.

5. **Keep emotions in check.** This one can feel very challenging, especially during a contentious discussion on a difficult topic. Being animated and fully engaged is just fine but be mindful when anger and frustration bubble to the surface and work hard to keep these emotions in check.

6. **Social media is not conducive to civil discussions.** I received a phone call that resulted in a ninety-minute discussion on a tough topic. We vetted the contentious topic thoroughly from all angles in a calm and respectful manner. A frustrated tweet or angry Facebook post will only invite vitriol and a series of "gotcha" comments. Get on the phone or meet in person if at all possible!

7. **Sometimes we have to be courageous**. The call I received was an act of courage. This man had no idea how I would react or the outcome of our conversation. It will take increased acts of courage like this and more of us bravely stepping up if we are going to tilt the scales back toward civility.

I am not the expert on civility and need to work on this like many of us. I believe, as I hope you will agree, that we have more in common with one another than we are often willing to admit. Let's sit down and calmly reason together rather than assume the worst of one another. If someone disagrees with us, we have an opportunity to listen, share, thoughtfully persuade them, or maybe just agree to disagree—and hopefully not get frustrated, become angry, and walk away. Our anger and frustration should *never* lead to breaking the law or violence of any kind. As I've mentioned before, G.K. Chesterton said it best: "We men and women are all in the same boat upon a stormy sea. We owe to each other a terrible and tragic loyalty."

Fostering greater civility at work, home, and the community starts with you and me. Let's embrace the challenge.

After reading this chapter, consider how you view the level of civility around you. How can you make a difference in promoting civility over the next few weeks? What will you do differently?

Conclusion

I'm very concerned that our society is much more concerned with information than wonder, in noise rather than silence. How do we encourage reflection? . . . Oh my, this is a noisy world.

MISTER ROGERS

I wrote the conclusion for *Upon Reflection* about a month before the book's publication after waking up early on a Saturday morning to gaze at a stunning sunrise in the Blue Ridge Mountains of Georgia from the back porch of a house my family rented for a summer weekend getaway. In the predawn light, the sun gradually rose from behind the mountains in front of me and cast its beautiful light on the scattered clouds in hues of orange and purple before it fully emerged with all its intense brilliance. The only noise I heard was the chatter of birds as I sipped my coffee and let my mind wander while I pondered this gift from our Creator. It was the perfect time and place to reflect on the book and life in general.

I have been on an intentional journey to more fully embrace the practice of reflection for the last several years, but the path has often been difficult and filled with obstacles. We are easily caught up in the daily grind of work racing from meeting to meeting like hamsters on a flywheel, and our lives outside of work are often equally as busy. We are surrounded by noise and distractions, and quiet moments are rare. We don't experience often enough the moments of peace and beauty like the one I described in the first paragraph. The smartphone, computer, and TV screens we gaze at all day long can become electronic pacifiers if we are not careful, and I fear we are at risk of morphing into tragic creatures resembling Gollum from *The Lord of the Rings* as he looks with obsessive longing at his "Precious." Think I am exaggerating? Try going twenty-four hours with no screen time of any kind and see how your brain reacts.

Every word in this book with its various and eclectic mix of topics was written through the prism of my own reflective thinking over the last few years. If you are willing to introduce more reflection time into your life, I encourage you to carefully ponder the various chapters you have just read. You might want to go back and reread the ones that resonated most, and I encourage you to do the action/challenge I pose at the end of each chapter. Here are **three additional ideas** to consider that will also help you to foster the practice of reflection:

1. **Be intentional about creating boundaries during the workweek.** Don't let your workdays be a continuous series of back-to-back meetings and other task-related activities without creating small windows of protected time set aside for deeper thinking, exercise, reading, listening to music, time with friends and loved ones, or anything else that gives you energy. Consider waking up a little earlier each day and use that quiet time for prayer or meditation. Schedule this time and protect it

as you would your most important business meetings and don't allow nonessential busywork to creep in. This practice not only promotes reflection but also helps avoid burnout.

2. **Go device free from time to time.** I know it is difficult in today's connected world, but turn off the screens every now and then. Put away the smartphone and shut down the computer more often, especially during non-work hours. Call a colleague—or even better, meet them in-person—rather than send an email. Read a book instead of watching TV. Experience the outdoors, even if you only take a walk in your neighborhood. A great start is to establish small device-free zones each day, such as early morning, lunchtime and dinnertime, and then expand from there. It will feel uncomfortable at first, but I encourage you to commit to replacing a portion of your screen time with something healthy, natural, and real.

3. **Spend quality in-person time with others.** Have a drink with an old friend or coffee with a business colleague. Go to sporting events with your kids. Savor meals with family and friends. Join other volunteers and give your time to a worthy cause. Take long walks with your significant other. Go on fun trips. Real in-person conversations or even quiet moments with the significant people in your life offer a much-needed respite from the noise and craziness of the world. This also helps you create memorable moments upon which to reflect.

Why does reflection matter? Why is it important? If you create space and time for this deeper thinking, it will absolutely help you lead a richer and fuller life. Reflection time is not only good for your mental and physical health—it will help you become a better human being. You will be more keenly aware of your surroundings and the different people you encounter each day, and you will recognize more clearly the opportunities you have to make a positive difference in this world. The last section of this book is filled with examples of the kindness and goodness of others that I may not have easily noticed before I began this journey years ago to more intentionally practice reflection.

I knew when I wrote *Upon Reflection* that it would be a little countercultural. Learning from the past . . . being more fully present in the moment . . . focusing on being good human beings. . . . These ideas may seem alien in today's world and out of sync with the culture, but that is exactly why I took the time to write this book and share it with you. No matter where you are in your career and whatever generation you belong to, I believe you will benefit from the advice and lessons you have read—and hopefully increase your own practice of reflection.

I am truly grateful to you for reading the book, and I hope it makes a positive difference in your life and how you engage with the world.

Thank you.

After reading this book, how will you more intentionally create opportunities for reflection in your life?

Acknowledgments

Upon Reflection is one of my favorite books, but it is also possibly my most surprising book. After finishing *Essential Wisdom for Leaders of Every Generation* in the summer of 2021, I had no immediate plans to write a new book. After *Essential Wisdom* was published, however, I began to write a series of posts on various experiences in my life and the lessons I have gleaned from them. I noticed over time that these posts all seemed to be tied together by the powerful theme of reflection, and before I knew it, I had written most of the book you have just read.

As I have grown older and more reflective, my sense of gratitude has grown as well. First and foremost, I thank God for the life He has given me, for my wonderful family, and for the opportunity to do work I love every single day. I am also grateful beyond measure for the opportunities in my life to experience the beauty of His creation as I described inadequately in various reflective moments in the book. I am grateful to my wonderful wife, Sandra, for always being there for me and for her unwavering love and support. I would be lost without her. I am grateful for my sons, Alex and Ryan, and the daily privilege of being their father. Many of the experiences and lessons I shared in this book are the fruits of the life we have all made together, and I can't thank them enough.

I thank my father, Steve, and my mother, Sandi, for the tremendous influence they have had on my life. They both have positively impacted me in countless ways, and I am truly grateful.

I appreciate the numerous experiences I have had with friends, work colleagues, clients, and sometimes complete strangers and what they have taught me over the years. I did my best to capture many of these stories in the book.

I am so appreciative of Karen Daniel and our longstanding partnership and friendship, and for the book cover and interior art design for this book and others over the years. Thank you to Claudia Volkman for her partnership, expert editing, and willingness to push me when I need it. To all who reviewed the book, offered helpful suggestions, and gave recommendations, please know that I am truly grateful.

Finally, I offer my sincere gratitude to Our Lady, *Stella Maris* (Star of the Sea). Thank you for guiding wandering travelers who may have lost their way and for accompanying me on the journey to write this book. You have been the North Star pointing the way forward in my life.

About the Author

Randy Hain is the founder and president of Serviam Partners (ServiamPartners.com) and the co-founder of the Leadership Foundry (MyLeadershipFoundry.com). With a successful thirty-plus-year career in senior leadership roles, corporate talent, and executive search, he is a sought-after executive coach for senior leaders at some of the best-known companies in the United States who are seeking expert guidance on identifying and overcoming obstacles to their success or developing new leadership skills. He is also an expert at onboarding and cultural assimilation for senior leaders as well as helping senior leadership teams improve trust, clarity, collaboration, and candid communication. Randy also offers consulting and coaching for companies, teams, and individual business leaders looking to develop more authentic and effective business relationships both inside and outside their organizations. His deep expertise in business relationships is a true area of differentiation for him and Serviam Partners.

He is an active community leader and serves on the board of Growing Leaders (www.GrowingLeaders.com). As a member of the advisory board for the Brock School of Business at Samford University, Randy frequently presents on relevant business and career topics to the Samford students. He is passionate about promoting autism awareness and advocating for adults with autism in the workplace. He is also an active member of St. Peter Chanel Catholic Church. Randy has earned a reputation as a creative business partner and generous thought leader through his books, articles, and speaking engagements.

Randy is the award-winning author of eight other books, including *Essential Wisdom for Leaders of Every Generation*, *Something More: The Professional's Pursuit of a Meaningful Life*, *LANDED! Proven Job Search Strategies for Today's Professional*, and *Special Children, Blessed Fathers: Encouragement for Fathers of Children with Special Needs*, all available on Amazon.

Learn more about Randy Hain's professional work, books, blog posts, and thought leadership at his website:

www.ServiamPartners.com

Made in the USA
Columbia, SC
10 April 2023

15177785R00102